MODULAR MATHS

John Connor JP BSc
Headmaster of Hale Preparatory School
and
Patricia Soper BSc

Dedicated to
the past, present and future
pupils of Hale Preparatory School

ORIFLAMME PUBLISHING

O 948093 07 2

First Edition 1990

Oriflamme Publishing Ltd
60 Charteris Road London N4 3AB

Phototypeset in 12 point Century Schoolbook
by Saxon Printing, Derby
and printed in the British Isles by
the Guernsey Press Co. Ltd.

INTRODUCTION

The text consists of 38 modules, each module comprising three sections:-

        Section A – Mechanical

        Section B – Problem-solving

        Section C – Investigative mathematics

Section A includes questions based on the essential mechanical processes, arithmetical skills, and the basic terminology of mathematics. Topics include: number values, percentages; the four rules and their application to fractions, decimals, money, distance, time, weight and capacity.

Section B deals with the application of concepts to the solution of problems. It includes questions on: perimeter, area, volume, averages, time/distance/speed, ratio, unequal sharing, bases, percentages, unitary method, sets and Venn diagrams, factors, and problems involving fractions and decimals.

All the basic knowledge and the methods required to tackle successfully Sections A and B will be found in the companion volume to this title, *The Rules of Maths*.

Questions in Section C place little reliance on established mathematical theories. Rather they demand the development of skills of analysis and interpretation; logical deduction and extrapolation. The majority of the questions in this section can be successfully approached in a variety of ways.

The format of the book presents, therefore, a balance between the traditional elements of any sound mathematics curriculum, and modern thinking and developments. We believe that these two elements are interdependent, and equally essential.

The questions can easily be adapted to suit individual teaching styles, and the differing needs and requirements of individual pupils. It is appreciated that all teachers have their own approach, particularly in their emphasis in practical work, which has accordingly been excluded from the present work. Many questions from sections B and C can, however, readily be modified to a practical/experimental approach. A brief guide for teachers to questions on particular topics is provided at the end of the book. Answer leaflets are available from the publishers.

The subject content of this book has been extensively tried in the classroom. It has proved of immense value in the preparation of pupils for entrance to independent grammar schools at the age of eleven; for Common Entrance; and for significant sections not only of GCSE courses but also for parts of several professional examinations.

MODULE ONE

Section A

(1) Increase fifteen thousand and eighty four by six thousand five hundred and fifty six.

(2) What is the value of the digit underlined: 346,754 ?

(3) 976×79

(4) $987 \div 17$

(5) $8\frac{1}{4} + 2\frac{2}{3}$

(6) $9\frac{1}{3} - 3\frac{4}{5}$

(7) $2\frac{4}{9} \times 1\frac{7}{11}$

(8) $3\frac{8}{9} \div 2\frac{1}{3}$

(9) Express 0.2 as a percentage.

(10) $13.6 - 3.007$

(11) 5.49×2.4

(12) $16.04 \div 0.002$

(13) 15 hours 29 mins + 6 hours 43 mins

(14) 3 hours 13 mins – 1 hour 51 mins

(15) Express 3.4 km in cm.

(16) How many sevenths in 49 ?

(17) Find $\frac{3}{5}$ of 35.

(18) How many days are there altogether in June, July, August and September ?

(19) If A = 2, B = 4, C = 6, what letter equals 16 ?

(20) Add the first five prime numbers. Do not include 1 as a prime number.

Section B

(1) Alison discovered that she had spent $\frac{2}{5}$ of her money, leaving her with £21. What amount of money did she originally possess ?

(2) A rectangle's perimeter is 24 cm. If the length of one side is 8 cm, what is the area of the rectangle ?

(3) A radio cassette priced at £60.00 was reduced by 20% in a sale. How much money did this reduction amount to ?

(4) If seven apples cost 61 pence, find the cost of twenty one apples at the same price.

(5) A cuboid has measurements: 5 cm by 4 cm by 6 cm.
   Find: (a) the total surface area
          (b) the total length of all the edges
          (c) the volume of the cuboid.

(6) A pile of books is 56 cm high. This pile is divided into two smaller piles. If one of the smaller piles is 8 cm higher than the other, what is the height of each pile ?

4

Section C

(1) The number 12 can be called a "blue" number. This means it can be divided exactly by the sum of its digits.

So $1 + 2 = 3$, and 12 is exactly divisible by 3.

What are the "blue" numbers between 10 and 30 ?

(2) It is possible to write any number greater than two in several ways using only 1's and 2's.

For example, 4 may be expressed in three ways:

$1 + 1 + 1 + 1 = 4$
$1 + 1 + 2 = 4$
$2 + 2 = 4$

Write down all the ways in which 7 can be written as the sum of 1's and 2's.

(3) In a bag are placed 11 red balls, 10 blue balls and 9 yellow balls.
A pupil is blindfolded and is required to perform the following tasks:-

  (a) To pull out two red balls.
  (b) To pull out two balls of the same colour.
  (c) To pull out three balls of different colours.
  (d) To pull out all the blue balls.

In each case work out the smallest number of balls it is necessary to pull out in order to complete the task.

(4) A triangle is a shape consisting of three sides. In the following shape, how many different triangles can be found ?

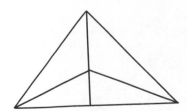

(5) A boy has a red dice and a blue dice. He throws both dice at the same time and finds that the two uppermost numbers add up to 8.
Write down the various ways this score could have been obtained.

(6) To find the distance round a circular racing track multiply its diameter by 3.142.
So the distance round a track of diameter 50 m =
$50 \times 3.142 = 157.10$ m.

With the help of the above information and the diagram on the right, work out the following:-

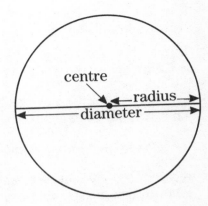

  (a) What is the distance round a track of radius 30 m ?
  (b) What is the distance round a track of diameter 68 m ?
  (c) If the distance round the track is exactly 219.94 m, find the diameter and radius of the track.

MODULE TWO

Section A

(1) Reduce ten thousand and one by four thousand six hundred and eighty nine.

(2) What must be added to 701 to make it exactly divisible by 19 ?

(3) 749×235

(4) $6^3/_4 + 2^1/_5$

(5) $7^1/_3 - 2^4/_7$

(6) $4^4/_5 \times 3^3/_4$

(7) $4^1/_2 \div 3^3/_8$

(8) $9.076 + 3.9$

(9) $3.7 - 1.009$

(10) 576×2.5

(11) $1.101 \div 0.03$.

(12) 9.4 km $+ 562$m (Give the answer in metres).

(13) £15.69×9

(14) Add the even numbers between 10 and 20.

(15) Find the volume of a cube of edge 2 cms.

(16) How many minutes are there between 9.15 a.m. and 1.05 p.m ?

(17) Reduce $13^1/_2$ to quarters.

(18) Find the value of 0.7 of £350.

(19) Express 24% as a fraction in its lowest terms.

(20) How many cm^3 equal $2m^3$?

Section B

(1) The perimeter of a square is 32 cm. What is the area of the square ?

(2) What is the area of the following shape ?

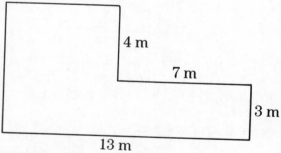

(3) Kate and Emma collected £64 in a collection for charity. Kate collected three times as much as Emma. How much did they each collect ?

(4) A dress originally priced at £80 was reduced by 20% in a sale. What was the sale price of the dress ?

(5) A car was travelling at a speed of 54 km/h. Express this speed in metres per second.

(6) In a group of 30 children, 17 children enjoy coffee and 18 enjoy tea. How many children enjoy: (a) both drinks, (b) only tea ?

6

Section C

(1) In the equation $12 \times 3 = 45$ some or all of the digits are in the wrong position.

Re-write the equation putting the digits in the correct order so making the equation correct.

(2) In the diagram on the right, x and y stand for single digit numbers. The numbers are such that any two of them add up to a number which is a perfect square. So $x + x$ is a perfect square number, as is $x + y$.

What numbers could be represented by x and y ?

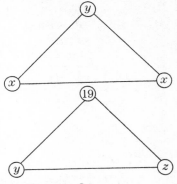

In this diagram, y and z represent different numbers. The numbers are such that any two of them add up to a perfect square. So $y + 19$ is a perfect square, as is $y + z$.

What numbers could be represented by y and z ?

(3) 3 and 5 are both prime numbers. The difference between the two numbers is 2.

Write down the prime numbers between 14 and 40 which also have a difference of 2.

(4) An amoeba divides into two separate amoebas every hour. How many amoebas will there be after five hours ?

(5) 16 and 149 are examples of "sen" numbers. They are called "sen" numbers because the digits, when added are exactly divisible by 7.

So, $16 = 1 + 6 = 7$, and $7 \div 7 = 1$.

In the same way, $149 = 1 + 4 + 9 = 14$, and $14 \div 7 = 2$.

Write down all the "sen" numbers between 20 and 100.

(6) When a square is divided in half to form two triangles, each of the triangles will be half the area of the original square.

Using this information, calculate the area of the triangle shown in the shape below.

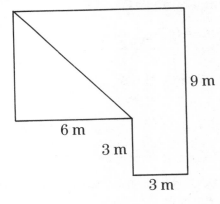

MODULE THREE

Section A

(1) What number is two thousand and six less than ten thousand two hundred and six ?

(2) What must be added to 710 to make it exactly divisible by 19 ?

(3) Reduce $13\frac{1}{2}$ to eighths.

(4) 976×349

(5) $6 \div 1,000$

(6) $8\frac{2}{3} + 6\frac{3}{4}$

(7) $9\frac{1}{7} - 2\frac{3}{5}$

(8) $3\frac{3}{8} \times 3\frac{1}{5}$

(9) $5\frac{1}{10} \div 1\frac{2}{5}$

(10) 9.74×3.6

(11) 9.007×0.2

(12) $3.912 \div 0.03$

(13) Express 45% as a fraction.

(14) 7 hours 17 mins − 3 hours 5 mins.

(15) How many degrees are there in: (a) a triangle, (b) a four sided figure, (c) a circle ?

(16) Find the cost of 100 tickets at £9.75 each.

(17) Find the full value of a painting if $\frac{6}{13}$ of its value is £180,000.

(18) (a) 3.67×10 (b) 4.978×100 (c) $397.4 \div 100$

(19) $(3.7 + 9.007) - 3.96$

(20) Find 0.7 of £400.

Section B

(1) After she had spent $\frac{5}{8}$ of her money, Alice found she had £15 left.
How much money did she originally have ?

(2) When 6.8 is added to a number and the result of this operation is divided by 0.03, the final answer is 350. What was the original number ?

(3) On a school holiday Peter spent three times more than Paul. If they spent £28 altogether, how much more money than Paul did Peter spend ?

(4) How many cubes of edge $\frac{1}{2}$ m will fit into the following cuboid ?

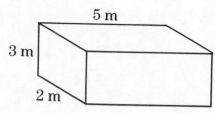

(5) For his "going home" presents at his party, Harry bought ten bags of sweets. Six had an average weight of 350 g and four had an average weight of 400 g.
What was the average weight of the bags ?

(6) Jack normally walks to school, a distance of 2.1 km, in twenty minutes.
How many metres does he walk in one minute ?

8

Section C

(1) Certain numbers are called "toc" numbers because they can be expressed as the sum of two prime numbers.

Examples of "toc" numbers are 33 and 34, because $2 + 31 = 33$ and $11 + 23 = 34$.

Which of the following numbers are "toc" numbers ?

$26, 31, 35, 37, 38, 41$

(2) All numbers have a "vibe". To find the "vibe" you first square the number and then add the digits of the result. For example, the "vibe" of 12 is 9, because $12 \times 12 = 144$ and $1 + 4 + 4 = 9$.

(a) Find the "vibe" of (a) 4 (b) 6

All "vibe" numbers are single digit numbers. If, after adding the digits, the answer remains two digits, then these must be added. For example the "vibe" number of 16 is 4, because $16 \times 16 = 256$ and $2 + 5 + 6 = 13$. Finally $1 + 3 = 4$.

(b) Find the "vibe" of: (a) 22 (b) 35

(3) To move from S to F a fly can only walk along a line and it can only travel vertically north or horizontally east.

In how many ways can a fly walk from S to F ?

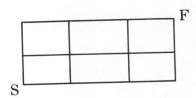

(4) A triangle is a shape comprising three straight lines. How many triangles can be drawn into these nine dots if the sides of the triangle can pass through any number of dots ?

● ● ●

● ● ●

● ● ●

(5) Each of the letters in the following addition sum represents a number. What number is represented by each letter ?

```
  A  B  6
  4  D  C+
  ‾‾‾‾‾‾‾
  D  6  1
```

(6) It takes three workmen 21 days to dig out a trench for a pipe.

(a) How long would it take six men who only work at $^3/_4$ of their rate to dig an identical trench ?

(b) How long would it take a mechanical digger to perform the same job, assuming it worked at seven times the rate of one of the original three men ?

MODULE FOUR

Section A

(1) If 13th July was a Monday, what was the day and date 90 days later ?

(2) Express one hundred and one thousand six hundred and ninety one in figures.

(3) $8^4/_5 + 2^3/_7$

(4) $10^1/_5 - 2^4/_7$

(5) $3^1/_9 \times 1^2/_7$

(6) $2^{13}/_{18} \div 1^5/_9$

(7) $49.074 + 9.097$

(8) $7.6 - 2.477$

(9) 39.67×2.5

(10) How many fours in 16 ?

(11) $8.112 \div 0.03$

(12) How many cm^3 in $5m^3$?

(13) Find the perimeter of a square of side 14 cm.

(14) How many cm^2 in $2^1/_2 m^2$?

(15) 7 hours 49 mins $\times$ 8

(16) How many times can 19 be taken from 763 ?

(17) Add the squares of 8 and 6.

(18) Find $12^1/_2\%$ of £1,600.

(19) Multiply the lowest prime number over 100 by the highest multiple of 3 less than 10.

(20) Give a two digit number whose unit digit is four times the ten digit ?

Section B

(1) Add the values of each of the numbers underlined: 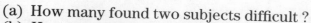 3.746 + 97.076 + 38.589

(2) John scored 28 marks out of a possible 40. Express his score as a percentage.

(3) Two books cost a total of £15.60. If one book cost £1.30 more than the other, how much did each book cost ?

(4) A postman delivering five parcels found that the average weight of the parcels was 3.4 kg. After delivering one parcel he found that the average weight of the parcels had fallen to 3.2 kg.

   How heavy was the parcel that he had delivered ?

(5) Ann drove to the station in 3 minutes at an average speed of 40 km/h. How long would it take her to walk the same distance at an average speed of 6 km/h ?

(6) The fourth year juniors in a school were asked to say which subjects they found difficult out of Maths., English and Science. Their replies are shown in the diagram.

   (a) How many found two subjects difficult ?
   (b) How many found maths difficult ?

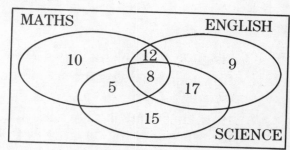

Section C

(1) Pat was always making discoveries. Her discoveries, however, were not always correct. Which of the following are *always* mathematically correct ?

    (a) Four is a factor of any number ending in two zeros.
    (b) All odd numbers, except 1, can be expressed as the sum of three consecutive numbers.
    (c) All the multiples of 5, except 5, can be expressed as the sum of five consecutive numbers.

(2) Consop discovered that if you continued to add the digits of square numbers until only one digit remained, then that digit itself would be a square number. He called this remaining square number a "Hale".
For example, the "Hale" of 49 is 4 because $4 + 9 = 13$ and $1 + 3 = 4$.

    (a) What is the "Hale" of 121 ?
    (b) What is the "Hale" of 625 ?
    (c) Sopcon proved that the theory is not always correct. Give one example when the theory is not correct.

(3) To find the "Damian" of a number of two digits, the digits are squared and the larger answer is subtracted from the smaller answer.
For example, the "Damian" of 23 is 5. This is worked out as follows:

$23 = 3^2 - 2^2 = 9 - 4 = 5$

    (a) Find the "Damian" of 54.
    (b) Find the "Damian" of 41.

If after the first subtraction the result is a two digit number, the process is repeated because all "Damian" numbers are of one digit.
For example, the "Damian" of 49 is 0. This is worked out as follows:

$49 = 9^2 - 4^2 = 81 - 16 = 65$

$65 = 6^2 - 5^2 = 36 - 25 = 11$

$11 = 1^2 - 1^2 = 1 - 1 = 0$

    (c) Find the "Damian" of 56. What do you notice about the "Damian" of 65 ?

(4) Rex was given four squares each of side 2 cm. He was required to form as many different shapes as possible by joining the squares together. However, he could only join the squares corner to corner.

For example:
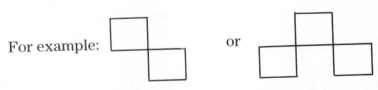
                                                   or

Draw as many shapes as possible using all four squares.

(5) In the grid on the right, place the numbers one to nine in such a way that every row adds up to a multiple of three.

11

MODULE FIVE

Section A

(1) $21^3/_4 + 5^5/_9$

(2) $5^1/_5 - 2^3/_4$

(3) $2^1/_{10} \times 11^2/_3$

(4) $2^{11}/_{12} \div 1^3/_4$

(5) $9.4 + 15.079$

(6) $13.97 - 2.007$

(7) 35.8×2.5

(8) $31.011 \div 0.02$

(9) Express 15% as a fraction.

(10) What is the value of 0.7 of 70 ?

(11) Add 3 hours 43 minutes and 5 hours 56 minutes.

(12) Express four hundred and one thousand eight hundred and nine in figures.

(13) Find the volume of a cake of edge 4 cm.

(14) A plane left Birmingham International at 11.35 a.m. and arrived at Rome Airport at 2.15 p.m. How long did the journey take ?

(15) Express 430,000 cm in km.

(16) 9 litres 25ml – 3 litres 75ml

(17) How many cm³ in 2m³ ?

(18) £39.75 × 29

(19) What is the value of the figure underlined: 5<u>8</u>7, 876?

(20) 6 hours 17 mins – 4 hours 39 mins

Section B

(1) A picture 10 cm by 17 cm is placed in a frame. There is a $1^1/_2$ cm margin all the way round between the picture and the edge of the frame.

What area of the frame is not covered by the picture ?

(2) Six babies weighed an average of 3 kg at birth. Three other babies weighed an average of 3.5 kg and another weighed 4.5 kg.

What was the average weight of the babies ?

(3) For every 20p stamp she purchased, Ann bought three 15p stamps. If she spent £5.85 altogether, how many of each stamp did she buy?

(4) The perimeter of a rectangle was 96 cm. The length of the rectangle was three times its width. What was the area of the rectangle?

(5) The cost of a restaurant's basic meal was increased by 10% each year. Two years ago the meal cost £8.00. What is the present price?

(6) A cube has a volume of 125 cm². What is its total surface area ?

12

Section C

(1) 14 can be regarded as a "Derb" number because it can be expressed as the sum of two or more successive numbers.

Example: $2 + 3 + 4 + 5 = 14$. Therefore 14 is a "Derb" number.

Similarly 15 is a "Derb" number because $7 + 8 = 15$.

List the numbers between 1 and 20 which are *not* "Derb" numbers.

(2) In the following two addition sums, the digits are correct, but they are in the wrong places. Re-write both sums, putting the digits in the correct order:

    (a)   10   (b)   37

                18   12

           282   490

(3) How many different squares can be found in the following shape ?

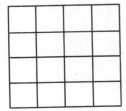

(4) The following two shapes can be defined as *identical* because one is simply the reflection of the other.

Draw as many different pairs of identical shapes as you can by using four squares of the same size.

(5) In the game of dominoes, each domino has two numbers printed on it, the numbers being expressed by dots. For example:

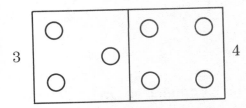

The numbers are $0 - 6$ inclusive. If each number can be used twice on the same domino, how many dominoes are there ?

MODULE SIX

Section A

(1) $3^3/_4 + 8^2/_3$

(2) $9^4/_5 - 2^7/_{10}$

(3) $2^7/_{10} \times 1^2/_3$

(4) $1^7/_8 \div 1^1/_4$

(5) $9.7 + 16.057$

(6) $19.3 - 3.09$

(7) 53.8×0.9

(8) $31.02 \div 0.3$

(9) 6 hours 39 minutes $\times$ 7

(10) $19 \div 100$

(11) 9 km 15 m $-$ 3 km 49 m

(12) £31.05 $\div$ 5

(13) Reduce eleven thousand and nine by two thousand six hundred and seven.

(14) How many fourths in 16 ?

(15) 3 litres 59 ml $-$ 1 litre 647 ml

(16) How many times can 23 be subtracted from 987 ?

(17) If 2 centimetres represent 1 km, how many cm² represent 1km² ?

(18) Which is the most likely weight of a pack of potatoes bought in a supermarket: 500 g., 1 kg., 5 kg., or 100 kg ?

(19) What is the total length of the edges of a cube if one edge equals 6 cms ?

(20) What is the date 60 days after 15th July ?

Section B

(1) Three books cost £8.00 each and two other books cost £3.00 each. What is the average cost of each book ?

(2) The diagram on the right shows a swimming pool. Around the pool runs a concrete path, shown by the shaded area. The path is exactly one metre wide.

Find the area of the path.

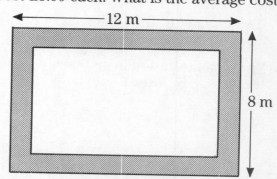

(3) Joyce and Vivienne found that their combined score in a test was 18. Joyce had obtained two more marks than Vivienne. What were the two scores ?

(4) In a group of 20 children, 12 enjoy television and 13 enjoy reading. What percentage of the children enjoy both television and reading?

(5) Thomas scored 18 marks out of a possible 40. Express this result as a decimal fraction.

(6) When $2^2/_3$ is added to a mixed number and the result is multiplied by $1^1/_5$, the final answer is $7^2/_5$.

What was the original mixed number ?

Section C

(1) This diagram represents a
rectangular dart board.
The points scored are shown
by the number in each section.

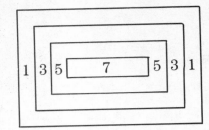

(a) In three hits is it possible to score an even number ?

(b) What is the least number of hits that will give you a score of exactly 27 ?

(c) How can a score of 41 be obtained without scoring 1 ?

(2) A palindromic number is a number whose digits when reversed give the same number.
Examples of palindromic numbers are 131, 2662 and 48784, since all give the same number
when the digits are written in reverse order.

(a) How many palindromic numbers are there between 1 and 100 ?

(b) Add the highest palindromic number less than 1,000 to the lowest palindromic number
greater than 100.

(c) What is the lowest palindromic five figure number ?

(3) The following graph represents a journey made by a cyclist:

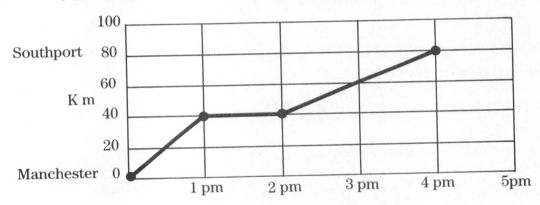

(a) What is the distance between Manchester and Southport ?

(b) How far from Manchester was the cyclist when he rested and how long did he rest for ?

(c) How long did the journey last ?

(d) What was the average speed of the journey ?

(4) Robert's calculator was not working correctly. As a result, addition became subtraction and
subtraction became addition. Adding 8 and 5 on the calculator gave an answer 3, whilst
subtracting 7 from 11 gave an answer 18. What answers would the calculator give to the
following:

(a) $8 - 7$
(b) $13 + 9$
(c) $(9 - 3) + 6$

(5) A number can be written as the sum of consecutive numbers. For example, 15 may be written
in two ways: $7 + 8 = 15$ and $4 + 5 + 6 = 15$. In the same way, 105 can be written as the sum of
consecutive numbers. Write down three ways in which this is possible.

15

MODULE SEVEN

Section A

(1) Express one hundred and one thousand six hundred and ten in figures.

(2) What must be added to 987 to make it exactly divisible by 17 ?

(3) $9.4 - 2.476$

(4) $8 \div 1,000$

(5) 3.4×1000

(6) 3 hours 46 mins + 2 hours 43 mins

(7) 9 km 15 m − 3 km 39 m.

(8) Find the volume of a cube of edge 2 cm.

(9) Find the total surface area of a cube of edge 3 cm.

(10) Express as fractions: (a) 0.3 (b) 38%

(11) Find 0.3 of 80.

(12) Find 45% of 400.

(13) What is the value of the figure underlined: 13.0$\underline{7}$6

(14) Is the length of a netball court approximately 3m, 30m, 300m or 3,000m ?

(15) How many sixths in $3^5/_6$?

(16) 5.3 km + 48 m

(17) A train left Manchester at 10.47 a.m. and arrived at its destination at 2.15 p.m. How many minutes did the journey take ?

(18) Express 20,000 cm in km.

(19) Add the first five multiples of 8.

(20) Add the prime numbers between 110 and 125.

Section B

(1) A piece of paper had a 2 cm border cut off all the way round. The paper then measured 14 cm by 18 cm. What was the original area ?

(2) $^1/_3$ of a post was painted red. $^5/_{12}$ of the post was painted yellow. The remaining 9 m was painted blue. What length was painted yellow ?

(3) Arthur bought an equal number of Mars Bars priced 20p and Twix Bars at 18p. If Arthur spent £3.42 altogether, how many Mars Bars did he buy ?

(4) Roy could row at a speed of 12 km/h in still water. He rowed for two hours against a current flowing at 4 km/h. He then rowed back to the starting point.
  (a) What distance did he row ?
  (b) What was the average speed of his journey ?

(5) Paul was half John's age. John was three times younger than Ann. If their combined ages totalled 36 years, how old was John ?

(6) In a week when he delivered milk every day, a milkman delivered a daily average of 976 bottles of milk for 5 days. On Saturday and Sunday the daily average was 901. What was the average weekly delivery ?

16

Section C

(1) To find the "Marck" of a number, that number is multiplied by the number one more than itself and the result divided by 2.

For example, the "Marck" of 8 is 36 because $8 \times 9 = 72$ and $72 \div 2 = 36$.

(a) What is the "Marck" of 13 ?

(b) What is the difference between the "Marcks" of 42 and 11 ?

(c) The "Marck" of a number is 210. What is the number ?

(2) When B is placed before a number of two or more digits, it means the digits are added. For example $B\,237 = 12$ because $2 + 3 + 7 = 12$. When BB is placed before a number it means the digits of the B of a number are added. For example $BB\,237 = 3$ because $2 + 3 + 7 = 12$ and $1 + 2 = 3$.

(a) Work out $B\,343$ and $BB\,795$

(b) $Bx = 11$. If x stands for a number between 120 and 130, what is the number ?

(c) A number between 160 and 175 has a BB of 6. What is the number ?

(3) A schoolboy devised the following dartboard:

Show how a score of 20 can be obtained in four hits without using the same number twice ?

(4) 128 schools entered a quiz competition. The quiz was organised on a knockout basis with the winning team going through to the next round.

(a) How many games did the winning team play?
(b) The average number of spectators watching each match was 74. How many spectators watched the entire competition ?

(5) The total number of degrees in the angles of a triangle is 180. In a rectangle the four angles are each 90 degrees.

(a) Using this information calculate the number of degrees represented by the letters x, y and t in the following diagram. (The two x's are equal).

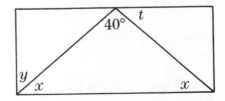

(b) Using a dotted line, draw in a line of symmetry.

MODULE EIGHT

Section A

(1) What must be added to 979 to make it exactly divisible by 18 ?

(2) Add the multiples of 7 between 20 and 40.

(3) Add the prime numbers between 30 and 40.

(4) $9^2/_3 + 6^3/_4$

(5) $10^1/_5 - 4^2/_3$

(6) $3^1/_9 \times 2^1/_4$

(7) $4^3/_8 \div 3^1/_2$

(8) 9.86 + 15.498

(9) 3.6 − 1.07

(10) 8.7 × 3.5

(11) 16.02 ÷ 0.03

(12) 9 hours 49 mins + 6 hours 53 mins

(13) 9 hours 17 mins − 3 hours 29 mins

(14) 9 hours 54 mins × 9

(15) 27 hours 54 mins ÷ 6

(16) 8 km 15 m − 3 km 29 m

(17) 9 km 15 m ÷ 5

(18) 10 m 13 cms − 2 m 46 cm

(19) 3.4 kg + 5 kg 54 g

(20) How many litres will a container of volume $3^1/_4$ m³ hold ?

Section B

(1) Calculate:

    (a) the perimeter, and
    (b) the area

of the shape shown
in the diagram.

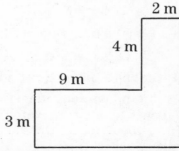

(2) A train left Exeter at 10.35 a.m. and arrived at Reading at 12.25 p.m. The average speed of the train was 120 km/h. How far did the train travel ?

(3) A junior school went to the theatre by coach. The number of children in the school would entirely fill coaches carrying 30, 35 or 42 passengers. What is the smallest possible number of children in the school ?

(4) A shopkeeper bought an article for £30 and sold it at a profit of $33^1/_3$%. What price did the article sell for ?

(5) A mast was 30 metres above the ground. If $^1/_6$ of the mast was embedded in the ground, what was the length of the mast ?

(6) A pool measures 18 metres in length and is 5 metres wide. It was decided to fill the pool to a depth of $1^1/_2$ metres. How long would it take to fill the pool if 3,000 litres of water entered the pool every hour ?

18

Section C

(1) A block of chocolate contains 24 small squares. The squares are arranged in four equal rows.

What is the lowest number of breaks necessary to split the block into 24 separate pieces ?

(2) 12 can be expressed in three different ways using the multiplication sign, namely $12 \times 1 = 12$, $6 \times 2 = 12$ and $3 \times 4 = 12$.

Write the ways 24 can be expressed in the same way.

(3) A piece of wood measuring 8 cm by 18 cm is cut into two pieces and reassembled into the shape of a square.

What are the measurements of the square ?

Sketch how the two pieces would be assembled.

(4) When a number is multiplied by another number ending in the same digit, and the answer also ends with that digit, the number is known as an "EAK" number.

For example $15 \times 15 = 225$.

Write down the numbers between 10 and 25 which become "EAK" numbers when multiplied by themselves.

(5) Two hundred and four pupils were asked whether they liked Maths, English and Science. Their answers were recorded in the following diagram.

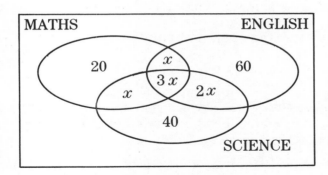

(a) What number of pupils is represented by x ?
(b) How many pupils like Maths ?
(c) How many pupils like two or more subjects ?
(d) How many don't like English ?
(e) Which is the most popular of these three subjects, and which is the least popular ?

MODULE NINE

Section A

(1) Reduce eleven million by sixteen thousand and one.

(2) Is the length of your classroom most likely to be 15, 150 or 1,500 metres?

(3) Would a Mars Bar be more likely to weigh 7g, 70g or 700g?

(4) What is the result of adding $\frac{1}{5}$ of 125 to the highest prime number less than 60?

(5) How many fourths in 56?

(6) If today is Friday 6th December, what will the day and date be 81 days hence?

(7) If a cube has a volume of 125 cm³, what will be the length of one edge?

(8) Which of the following figures are in the hundredths column: 12,893.569?

(9) 3 km + 437 m + 936 cm. Express your answer in metres.

(10) How many cm in 3.7 km?

(11) 13 litres 15 ml ÷ 5

(12) Add the odd square numbers between 1 and 130.

(13) 39.43 × 2.5

(14) 53 hours 36 mins ÷ 6

(15) Reduce 15 to fifths.

(16) How many cubic cm in 3¾ cubic metres?

(17) Find 0.3 of 90.

(18) 9 ÷ 1,000

(19) 6 hours 17 mins – 3 hours 49 mins

(20) What is the area of a piece of paper 21 cm by 15 cm?

Section B

(1) After six examination results, Janet's average mark was 58%. After the seventh result was announced her average mark had been increased by 2%.
What mark did she obtain in her seventh examination?

(2) In one of his examinations, Peter scored 31 out of a possible 40 marks.
What was his mark expressed as a percentage?

(3) Find (a) the total surface area, (b) the length of the edges of the following cuboid:

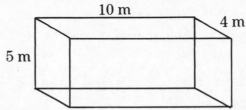

(4) A sprinter covered 100 metres in exactly 10 seconds. Express this speed in km/h.

(5) A group all enjoyed the cinema or the theatre as a leisure activity. Three quarters enjoyed the cinema and two thirds enjoyed the theatre. If 15 members enjoyed both the cinema and theatre, how many were in the group?

(6) 327 is added to a certain number and the result is then divided by 15. If the final answer is 30, what was the original number?

Section C

(1) An "Arthog" dartboard has 20 numbers from 1 to 20 and has no double or triple scores.

Pat only hit the dartboard with two darts and yet managed to score 32.

This score could have been achieved in a number of ways. List five of them.

(2) Put the numbers 1 to 9 in the following boxes so that no two consecutive numbers are next to each other either vertically or horizontally.

Note: 2 and 3 are consecutive numbers, as are 8 and 7.

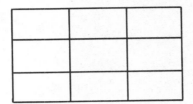

(3) Alison thought she had discovered a new mathematical theorem when she worked out that the difference between two consecutive square numbers is always a prime number.

For example, selecting 5 and 6: $5 \times 5 = 25$ and $6 \times 6 = 36$. The difference between 36 and 25 is 11, and 11 is a prime number.

Select four pairs of consecutive square numbers and test whether Alison's theorem is correct.

(4) The symbol [] stands for the greatest whole number less than the mixed number in the bracket. So $[6^{1}/_{3}] = 6$, $[8^{1}/_{2}] = 8$ and $[18] = 18$.
Work out the following:

(a) $\left[\dfrac{13^{1}/_{3}}{2^{1}/_{2}} \right]$ (b) $\left[\dfrac{[13^{1}/_{3}]}{2^{1}/_{2}} \right]$ (c) $\left[\dfrac{[13^{1}/_{3}]}{[2^{1}/_{2}]} \right]$

(5) To find the "geometric mean" of two numbers, first multiply the numbers together and then find a number which, when squared, gives the same result.

For example, the "geometric mean" of 4 and 9 is 6 because $4 \times 9 = 36$ *and* $6 \times 6 = 36$.

(a) Find the "geometric mean" of 3 and 48.

(b) The "geometric mean" of two numbers is 10. If one of the numbers is 25, what is the second number ?

(c) The "geometric mean" of two numbers is 8. If one number is four times larger than the other, what are the two numbers ?

(6) Mr Slade the mathematician had the job of adding together two sets of numbers to see if a certain theorem was correct. The first set had been provided by another mathematician, Consop, who worked in base ten. The second set, however, had been generated by his computer which operated on the binary system. The sets were as follows:

Set 1:   14   26   37
Set 2: 10010   1110   101001

(a) What answer did he send to Consop ?

(b) What answer did he feed into his computer ?

MODULE TEN

Section A

(1) Express two hundred and one thousand and ten in figures.

(2) $3.1 \times 1,000$

(3) $8\frac{3}{5} + 2\frac{4}{7}$

(4) $10\frac{1}{3} - 4\frac{3}{5}$

(5) $2\frac{5}{8} \times 2\frac{2}{3}$

(6) $5\frac{1}{2} \div 8\frac{1}{4}$

(7) $9.8 + 17.04$

(8) $5.4 - 1.097$

(9) 34.3×2.5

(10) $13.11 \div 0.03$

(11) Express $2\frac{1}{2}\%$ as a fraction.

(12) 17 hours 24 mins $\div$ 6

(13) How many cm^3 in $1\ m^3$?

(14) 15 litres 17 ml $-$ 2.35 litres

(15) Divide 1,000 in the ratio 3:2

(16) What is the value of the figure underlined: 93,497 ?

(17) How many times can 19 be taken away from 746 ?

(18) Add the square numbers between 100 and 200.

(19) Express 1745 in 12 hour clock time.

(20) How many minutes are there between 11.15 a.m. and 1.05 p.m ?

Section B

(1) John started off with £12. He spent a quarter of it, and then he spent one-third of what was left.

How much did he spend altogether ?

(2) Find the total surface area of a cuboid measuring 2 m by 3 m by 5 m.

(3) A centre-forward scored three times as many goals as the left-winger. If they scored 28 goals between them, how many goals did they each score ?

(4) A coat now priced £85 has been reduced by 15% in a sale. What was the original price of the coat ?

(5) A girl cycled for 3 hours at an average speed of 24 km/h, then a further 2 hours at an average speed of 34 km/h.

What distance did she cover and what was her average speed throughout the journey ?

(6) If $\frac{7}{8}$ of a number is 21, what is $\frac{3}{4}$ of the number ?

Section C

(1) To "dabble" a number is to halve it and multiply the result by 5. So, when 8 is "dabbled" the answer is 20 because 8 divided by 2 = 4 and $4 \times 5 = 20$.

(a) What is the result when 20 is "dabbled"?

(b) When a certain number is "dabbled", the final answer is 125. What is the original number?

(2) A group of 40 people were asked whether they liked tea and coffee. The replies made by the group are shown in the diagram below.

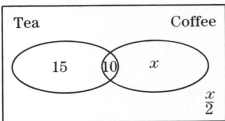

(a) How many people are represented by x?

(b) How many of the group like tea?

(c) How many of the group just like one drink?

(3) Tina spent 39 pence on sweets. She gave the shopkeeper a 50 pence coin. Write the ways in which she could have received her change.

(4) Horace the frog can only jump one stepping stone at a time. Moreover, he cannot jump in a backward direction or diagonally. If he has to jump from A to B, in how many different ways can he make the journey?

```
A x   x   x

    x   x   x

    x   x   x B
```

(5) Study the following series of numbers carefully noticing the pattern:

$$
\begin{aligned}
1 + 3 &= 2 \times 2 = 4 \\
1 + 3 + 5 &= 3 \times 3 = 9 \\
1 + 3 + 5 + 7 &= 4 \times 4 = 16 \\
1 + 3 + 5 + 7 + 9 &= 5 \times 5 = 25
\end{aligned}
$$

(a) Write down a similar series whose sum is 100

(b) 9 is the last number of the series whose sum is 25.
Write down the last number of a similar series whose sum is 169.

(c) Use the above method to work out $1 + 3 + 5 \ldots 37 + 39$.

23

MODULE ELEVEN

Section A

(1) Reduce $39\frac{1}{2}$ to halves.

(2) Find 37% of 600.

(3) What needs to be added to 817 to make it exactly divisible by 16 ?

(4) Increase two hundred and one thousand and six by sixty one thousand and fifty six.

(5) What is 0.1 of £12,000 ?

(6) How many fifths in $4\frac{2}{5}$?

(7) What is the value of each of the figures underlined:
(a) 36.00<u>7</u> (b) <u>9</u>68.874 (c) 3.07<u>5</u>

(8) 38 hours 36 mins ÷ 6

(9) Express $87\frac{1}{2}$% as a fraction.

(10) How many times is B smaller than A ? — $\dfrac{A \quad B}{77{,}777}$

(11) Express $1\frac{7}{20}$ as a decimal.

(12) How many cms^2 in 2m^2 ?

(13) $3\frac{1}{7} \div 2\frac{2}{21}$

(14) Find the total of the prime numbers from 10 to 20

(15) 9.08 ÷ 0.002

(16) $4\frac{3}{5} + 2\frac{3}{4}$

(17) 3.4 kg + 59 g

(18) What is the square of 14 ?

(19) What is the cost of 30 books at £5.74 each ?

(20) Find the value of 0.17 of 300.

Section B

(1) A field measures 35 m by 45 m. What is the perimeter of the field ?

Posts are placed round the field at 5 m intervals with one post at each corner. How many posts are required ?

(2) A bathroom floor measures 5 m by 3 m. The floor is completely covered with tile squares of edge half a metre. How many tiles are needed to cover the floor ?

(3) Last year a village's population increased by 10% to 330. What was its population before the increase ?

(4) John obtained twice as many house points as Joan, but Zoe obtained twice as many as John. The three children obtained a total of 49 points. How many did they each obtain ?

(5) The sum of two numbers is 180. The difference between the numbers is 40. What is the product of the two numbers ?

(6) Seven-twelfths of a post was painted green. The remaining 15 metres were painted yellow. What was the length of the post ?

Section C

(1) A milk crate left at a school is divided into four rows and six columns, as shown in the diagram below.

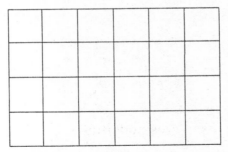

One day 18 bottles were left and it was discovered that each row and each column contained an even number of bottles.

Show how this could be achieved.

(2) Draw a circle. On the circle mark in four dots. Join each dot to the next dot with a straight line, thus forming a four-sided figure.

(a) How many diagonals can be drawn in the figure ?

(b) How many diagonals can be drawn in figures comprising

    (i) five dots
    (ii) six dots ?

(c) How many diagonals could be drawn if the figure comprised 50 dots ?

(3) 16 has five divisors namely 1, 2, 4, 8 and 16. These five numbers are called divisors because they all divide into 16.

How many divisors has (a) 24 and (b) 36 ?

(4) If you had never learned your tables it would be possible to answer questions by using addition.

So, for example 5×4 could be answered by adding 5 four times – that is $5 \times 4 = 20$, and $5 + 5 + 5 + 5 = 20$.

(a) Write down two addition sums that would allow you to work out 7×5.

(b) What kind of table question can only be answered by one addition sum ?

A boy takes one second to add two numbers and six seconds to multiply two numbers.

(c) How much time would the boy save by multiplying 9×8 rather than working out the sum by addition ?

(d) Which would be the fastest way for the boy to work out 6×5 ?

MODULE TWELVE

Section A

(1) $4^3/_5 + 5^3/_7$

(2) $18^1/_3 - 2^4/_7$

(3) $1^2/_5 \times 2^1/_7$

(4) $3^1/_2 \div 2^5/_8$

(5) $3.4 - 1.003$

(6) 9.37×3.5

(7) $38.02 \div 0.002$

(8) $837 \div 19$

(9) 986×757

(10) What is $^7/_{19}$ of 57 ?

(11) Express the speed of 90 km/h as a speed in metres per second.

(12) What is the value of the figure underlined: 3.0<u>7</u>9 ?

(13) How many sixths in 36 ?

(14) Find 35% of £80.

(15) Find the perimeter of the square of side 15 cm.

(16) What is the one prime number between 120 and 130.

(17) 3.4 kg $+ 96$ g

(18) Add 0.4 of 60 to $^7/_8$ of 72.

(19) How many minutes between 11.50 a.m. and 3.15 p.m ?

(20) Add the square numbers between 50 and 100.

Section B

(1) One-eighth of a group had red hair. Two-sevenths of the remainder had fair hair. The other 35 members of the group had dark hair. How many were in the group ?

(2) The length of a cuboid is 8 cm and its width 6 cm. If the total length of the edges equals 76 cm, what is the height of the cuboid ?

(3) Express a speed of 15 m per second in km/h.

(4) The pupils at a certain school would not believe their maths teacher when he told them that he was 213 years old.
In fact he was telling the truth – but in base five.
How old was the teacher in base ten ?

(5) Two ski jumps made by the Olympic champion totalled 224 m. If one of the jumps was 10 m shorter than the other, what was the length of the longer jump ?

(6) A kitchen measured 2.75 m by 7.25 m. It was to be covered in square tiles. What was the largest size of tile that could be used if only complete tiles were to be used ? How many of these tiles were needed ?

Section C

(1) The floor of a hall was to be covered with carpet squares.
The hall itself was also square.

The carpet fitter completed the two diagonals of the hall first.

If he needed 41 carpet squares to complete the two diagonals, how many squares did he need to finish the entire hall ?

(2) In the following division sum, the digits 1, 2, 3, 4, and 6 are each used once. There is no remainder. Fill in the digits in the appropriate places.

$$\frac{\quad 5\ D}{Q\,|A\ B\ C}$$

(3) There are eight square numbers containing one or two digits.
What are they ?

Which three digit square number can be made
either by putting a one digit square number in front of a two digit square number
or by putting a two digit square number in front of a one digit square number ?

(4) In the series of numbers 3, 7, 11, 15 . . . each number is four more than the number before it.

  (a) Give the next three numbers.
  (b) The twentieth number is 79. What is the sixteenth number ?
  (c) What is the hundredth number in the series ?
  (d) In the series 5, 9, 13, 17 . . . what is the thousandth number ?

(5) Study the following pattern carefully:

$$1 \times 2 \qquad\qquad = \quad \tfrac{1}{3} \times 1 \times 2 \times 3$$
$$1 \times 2 + 2 \times 3 \qquad = \quad \tfrac{1}{3} \times 2 \times 3 \times 4$$
$$1 \times 2 + 2 \times 3 + 3 \times 4 = \quad \tfrac{1}{3} \times 3 \times 4 \times 5$$

  (a) Write down the next line, and then check your answer by working out both sides.

  (b) Write down the last product on the left side, if the right side reads:- $\tfrac{1}{3} \times 20 \times 21 \times 22$.

  (c) Write down the right side if the last product on the left side reads:- 40×41.

(6) John was set a mathematics assignment to work out a series of denary (base 10) numbers in base two. However, he did not read the instructions correctly, and instead worked out all the numbers in base 5.

For the first number John gave his answer as 102.

  (a) What (base ten) number did he start with ?
  (b) What should his correct answer in base two have been ?

The answer for the second number should have been 110001.

  (a) What was the original number ?
  (b) What answer would John have obtained ?

The third number in the series was 103.

  (a) What would be the correct answer for this number ?
  (b) What number would John obtain as the answer ?

MODULE THIRTEEN

Section A

(1) Express 31,957 to the nearest hundred.

(2) $11^3/_5 + 6^3/_4$

(3) What must be added to 579 to make it exactly divisible by 17 ?

(4) Reduce a hundred and nine thousand by eighty nine.

(5) $5^1/_3 - 2^3/_4$

(6) $3^8/_9 \times 5^2/_5$

(7) $3^1/_7 \div 2^5/_{14}$

(8) $9.7 - 1.097$

(9) $3.46 + 937.9$

(10) 46.37×0.32

(11) $9.08 \div 0.002$

(12) Express $^{17}/_{20}$ as a decimal.

(13) Express $62^1/_2$% as a fraction in its lowest terms.

(14) Express $^3/_5$ as a percentage.

(15) Reduce 3.2 km to metres.

(16) 13 hours 36 mins $\div$ 6

(17) How many mm^2 in 2cm^2 ?

(18) Add the prime numbers between 80 and 90.

(19) Reduce 25 to fifths.

(20) Add the even square numbers between 100 and 400.

Section B

(1) John spent one-third of his money, then he spent half of the remainder.
If he ended up with £8, how much did he start off with ?

(2) The measurements of a room are 5.3 m by 3.75 m.
Find (a) the area (b) the perimeter of the room.

(3) Three girls compared their maths examination results. Emma had twice as many as Alison, but only half the marks of Katie. If they obtained 112 marks altogether, how many marks did they each obtain ?

(4) A container measuring 5 m by 4 m was filled to a depth of 1 m with water.
If one litre is the equivalent to one thousand cubic centimetres, how many litres of water were in the container ?

(5) A car travelled 200 km at an average speed of 50 km/h and then returned over the same distance in six hours.
What was the average speed of the entire journey ?

(6) A farmer has sufficient fodder to keep 35 cows for 50 days.
If he sold seven cows, how long would the same amount of fodder last ?

Section C

(1) In the following pattern the last number in each row is called a triangular number.

$$
\begin{array}{ccccc}
\mathbf{1} & & & & \\
2 & \mathbf{3} & & & \\
4 & 5 & \mathbf{6} & & \\
7 & 8 & 9 & \mathbf{10} & \\
11 & 12 & 12 & 14 & \mathbf{15}
\end{array}
$$

   (a) What is a triangular number ?

   (b) What are the next two triangular numbers ?

   (c) What type of number always results if two consecutive triangular numbers are added together ?

(2) Lillian developed a system of finding square numbers.

First, a pair of consecutive odd numbers is chosen.
Secondly, the numbers are multiplied and 1 is added to the result.
Finally, the result is divided by 4.

For example, if 13 and 15 are selected:

$15 \times 13 = 195 \qquad 195 + 1 = 196 \qquad 196 \div 4 = 49$
Since $7 \times 7 = 49$, 49 is a square number.

Prove the "Lill" system by selecting two consecutive odd numbers between 20 and 30. Check your answer.

(3) In the following two multiplication sums, a number of digits have been replaced by letters. What are the missing digits ?

   (a)
$$
\begin{array}{r}
\text{A } 7 \\
9 \\
\hline
4 \text{ B } 3
\end{array}
$$
   (b)
$$
\begin{array}{r}
6 \text{ D} \\
\text{E} \\
\hline
3 \text{ F } 4
\end{array}
$$

(4) How many separate *regions* are to be found in the following diagram ?

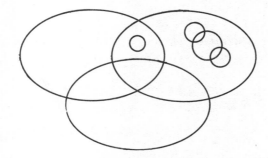

(5) The "geek" of two numbers is calculated in the following way.
The "geek" of 5 and 12 is 13 because:
$(5 \times 5) + (12 \times 12) = 25 + 144 = 169$, and $\underline{13} \times \underline{13} = 169$

Therefore, it can be stated: "geek" 6, 8 = 10

   (a) Calculate "geek" 3, 4
   (b) If the "geek" x, 20 = 25, what number does x stand for ?

MODULE FOURTEEN

Section A

(1) How many times can 19 be subtracted from 978 ?

(2) Express 10,976 to the nearest 100.   (3) 7 hours 49 mins × 7

(4) What is the value of the figure underlined: 84.9$\underline{7}$6 ?

(5) 6 hours 17 mins − 3 hours 39 mins

(6) 5 hours 39 mins + 3 hours 46 mins

(7) 9 hours 36 mins ÷ 6   (8) $3\frac{3}{4} + 6\frac{2}{3}$

(9) $10\frac{1}{3} - 4\frac{3}{5}$ (10) $4\frac{3}{8} \times 3\frac{1}{5}$

(11) $3\frac{1}{9} \div 5\frac{1}{6}$ (12) 5.46 + 39.007

(13) 5.4 − 1.742   (14) Reduce $15\frac{3}{4}$ to quarters.

(15) Is the length of a football field likely to be 100, 1,000 or 10,000 m ?

(16) If today is 15th July, what will be the date in 84 days time ?

(17) Add the lowest prime number more than 105 to the highest odd number less than 104.

(18) If A = 5 and B = 6, evaluate: (a) 3A   (b) 4B   (c) 5(A + B)

(19) 17 ÷ 100   (20) What is 8^2 ?

Section B

(1) The sum of two numbers is 340. The difference between the numbers is 28.
What are the two numbers ?

(2) A sweater was sold for £6. This price was the result of an 80% reduction from the original price. What was the original price ?

(3) In a clearance sale, 17 golf balls were sold for £17.73. What would be the cost of 51 balls at the same price ?

(4) Peter ran a distance of 45 km at an average speed of 15 km/h.
He then returned to his starting point in 6 hours.
What was the average speed of the entire journey ?

(5) A square of area 64 cm² is made into a rectangle of the same perimeter.
If the length of the rectangle is 10 cm, what is the area of the rectangle ?

(6) Using the digits 8, 3, 9 and 7 once, make the highest possible even number and from it, subtract the lowest odd number which can be made, again using each digit only once.

Section C

(1) 5 is said to be a "jon" number because it is the sum of two square numbers:

$$1^2 = 1 \times 1 = 1 \text{ and } 2^2 = 2 \times 2 = 4 \text{ and } 1 + 4 = 5.$$

State three "jon" numbers between 20 and 30.

(2) In mini-snooker, a red ball must be potted before another colour is potted.
A red ball scores 1 point, black scores 7, pink scores 6,
blue scores 5 and brown scores 4.
There are ten balls of each colour on the table.

  (a) What is the maximum score that could be achieved in six shots ?
  (b) How could 46 points be scored in the least number of shots ?
  (c) How can a score of 28 be achieved ?

(3) Fill in the following squares so that the second row is double the first row and the third row is three times the first row. Each square contains only one digit.

2		3
		6
	1	

(4) To "hog" one number with another is to find the remainder when their product is divided by 7.
The symbol * between two numbers indicates they are going to be "hogged".
Thus, $5 * 10 = 1$ because $5 \times 10 = 50$ and $50 \div 7 = 7 \text{ remainder } 1$.

  (a) Calculate 15 * 9
  (b) If $x * 4 = 3$, what is the lowest value of x ?
  (c) Find all the single-digit numbers which, when "hogged" with themselves, give 4.

(5) When an odd number of consecutive numbers are added together, the middle number in the series of consecutive numbers can be found by dividing the total by the number of consecutive numbers.
For example, if five consecutive numbers are added, and the result is 95, then the middle number in the series will be $95 \div 5 = 19$.
From this the other numbers in the series can be worked out: $17+18+19+20+21$

  (a) If seven consecutive numbers total 70, what is the first number in the series ?

  (b) If the middle number of a series of nine numbers is 15, what is the total of the numbers in the series ?

  (c) If the middle number in a series of 41 numbers is 101, what is the total of the numbers in the series ?

MODULE FIFTEEN

Section A

(1) $9^2/_3 + 3^4/_5$

(2) $8^1/_3 - 2^3/_5$

(3) $9^3/_4 \times 1^3/_{13}$

(4) $7^4/_5 \div 1^3/_{10}$

(5) $3.7 - 1.09$

(6) $15.6 - 12.07$

(7) 37.6×7.3

(8) $19.011 \div 0.3$

(9) $987 \div 23$

(10) $19 \div 1,000$

(11) 15 hours 36 mins $\times$ 8

(12) 3.4 km $-$ 56 m

(13) Express one million, one thousand and one in figures.

(14) If A = 6 and B = 8, calculate: (a) A + B (b) AB (c) $^A/_B$

(15) 3.59 litres $-$ 1 litre 59 ml

(16) How many halves in $14^1/_2$?

(17) Add the prime numbers between 25 and 35. (18) $7^2 - 6^2$

(19) In the number 93474, put in a decimal point to make the digit 7 have a value of $^7/_{100}$

(20) How many more minutes did the year 1988 have than the year 1989 ?

Section B

(1) Five examination results averaged 60%. When the worst result was omitted the average increased to 65%. What was the worst result ?

(2) A piece of paper 20 cm by 12 cm had a margin of 1 cm cut off all the way round. What fraction of the original remained ?

(3) When 3.6 is added to a number and the result is multiplied by 2.1 the final answer is 12.81. What was the original number ?

(4) In a survey, it was found that out of every 100 television viewers, three enjoyed sports programmes for every two that disliked them.

Express as a percentage the number that enjoy sports programmes.

(5) In a group of 40 children, 22 enjoy television and 23 enjoy reading. What fraction of the children enjoy both reading and television ?

(6) A personalised stereo is reduced from £40 to £22. What percentage reduction is this ?

Section C

(1) John's calculator was not working correctly. All multiplications became divisions and all divisions became multiplications. As a result 15×3 became 5, and 7 divided by 5 became 35.

What answers would his calculator give for the following ?

(a) 16×4 (b) 36×6 (c) $18 \div 3$ (d) $(15 \times 5) \div 20$

(2) In maths, flow charts are sometimes used. The flow charts are always self-explanatory.

$x \rightarrow$ $\boxed{+3}$ $\rightarrow$ $\times 4$ $\rightarrow$ F

In the above flow chart, if x is given a specific value, then F may be worked out.

For example, let $x = 5$

$5 \rightarrow$ $\boxed{+3}$ $\rightarrow$ $\times 4$ $\rightarrow 32$

Find x in the following:

(a) $x \rightarrow$ $\boxed{+5}$ $\rightarrow$ $\boxed{\times 4}$ $\rightarrow 44$

(b) $10 \rightarrow$ $\boxed{+x}$ $\rightarrow$ $\boxed{\times 3}$ $\rightarrow 51$

(c) $14 \rightarrow$ $\boxed{-2}$ $\rightarrow$ $\boxed{\div 4}$ $\rightarrow x$

(d) $9 \rightarrow$ $\boxed{+11}$ $\rightarrow$ $\boxed{\div x}$ $\rightarrow 3^{1}/_{3}$

(3) A greengrocer built up a pile of cans in the shape of a triangular pyramid. The top can was built on two cans below it. These two cans in turn fitted into the spaces of the three cans below them and so on. The greengrocer worked this out mathematically.

1 layer   = 1 can
2 layers   = $1 + 2 = 3$ cans
3 layers   = $1 + 2 + 3 = 6$ cans

(a) How many cans would there be with (i) 4 layers   (ii) 7 layers ?

(b) If he put 120 cans in the pile, how many layers would the pile have ?

(4) If the digits of a number are added, the result is its digit sum, which is always one digit. This means that if the result of adding the digits is a two digit answer, the process must be repeated.

For example: 9 8 5 6 becomes $9 + 8 + 5 + 6 = 28$ (first digit sum)
Then: 2 8 = $2 + 8 = 10$ (second digit sum)
Finally: $1 + 0 = 1$
Therefore 1 is the final digit sum of 9856

Find the final digit sum of: (a) 9857   (b) 8997

(5) Alan and Tom play cards and always stake 10p on each game. At the end of the evening Alan had won three games and Tom had won 30p. What is the least number of games they could have played during the evening ?

MODULE SIXTEEN

Section A

(1) 374×216

(2) What is 0.1 of £1,000 ?

(3) Increase two hundred and one thousand and six by one thousand and fifty six.

(4) How many times can 16 be taken from 817 ?

(5) $8\frac{1}{3} - 2\frac{4}{7}$

(6) $9\frac{4}{5} \times 2\frac{1}{7}$

(7) $8\frac{1}{3} + 2\frac{4}{7}$

(8) $9.8 + 16.75$

(9) $36.5 - 2.076$

(10) 38.7×3.5

(11) $38.61 \div 0.003$

(12) $4\frac{4}{9} \div 3\frac{1}{3}$

(13) Find the cost of 425 books at £2.60 each.

(14) Find 37% of 600.

(15) How many fifths in $4\frac{2}{5}$?

(16) What is the value of the figure underlined: 37.0$\underline{9}$8 ?

(17) 9.3 km $+ 4$ km 56 m

(18) 9 km 15 m $- 3$ km 45 m

(19) How many minutes between 10.15 a.m. and 2.20 p.m ?

(20) 17 km 15 m $\div 5$

Section B

(1) $5\frac{1}{3}$ is added to a mixed number. The result of this operation is multiplied by $1\frac{1}{11}$. If the final answer is $9\frac{10}{11}$, what was the original mixed number ?

(2) If 0.19 of a number is 76, what is the number ?

(3) A car's price was reduced by 15% to £11,900. What was the price of the car before the reduction ?

(4) In a long-jump competition, Mary and Kath jumped a combined length of 4.8 m. If Mary jumped 28 cm longer than Kath, how far did Kath jump ?

(5) The average mark scored by 20 boys in a test was 15. The average mark scored by ten girls was 18. What was the average mark of the whole group ?

(6) A school's pupils could be divided into groups of 25, 30 or 45. What is the lowest possible number of pupils in the school ?

Section C

(1) Put the numbers 1 to 6 into the following squares so that adjacent numbers such as 1 and 2, or 5 and 4 go into squares that are not joined by a straight line.

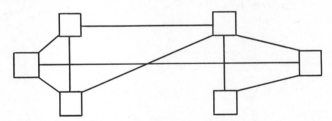

(2) If x represents the same number in each fraction, complete the statement:

$$\frac{x}{x} - \frac{x}{6} = \frac{x}{12}$$

(3) The number 12 is exactly equal to four times the sum of its digits.

That is, $1 + 2 = 3$ and $4 \times 3 = 12$.

Find numbers which are:

(a) exactly equal to four times the sum of their digits, when the numbers are greater than 20

(b) exactly equal to twice the sum of their digits

(c) exactly equal to three times the sum of their digits.

(4) If 4 and 9 are added, the answer is 13 which is a prime number.

4 and 9 are consecutive square numbers.

Select your own examples and show whether the addition of two consecutive square numbers always results in a prime number.

(5) The "required" answer of a number is obtained when the number is multiplied by one more than itself and then the result is then multiplied by 2.

For example, the "required" answer of 7 is 112 because $7 \times 8 = 56$ and $56 \times 2 = 112$.

(a) What is the "required" answer of 5 ?
(b) Work out the difference between the "required" answers of 9 and 8.
(c) The "required" answer of a number is 264. What is the number ?

(6) When 2 numbers are "linked" signified by a * the first number is trebled and is then multiplied by $\frac{1}{2}$ the second number.

For example $9 * 20 = 270$ because $9 \times 3 = 27$, $20 \div 2$ is 10, and $27 \times 10 = 270$.

Calculate
(a) $14 * 8$
(b) $30 * 100$

Find the values of x in the following

(c) $x * 40 = 720$
(d) $24 * x = 1440$.

MODULE SEVENTEEN

Section A

(1) How many times can 23 be subtracted from 917 ?

(2) Find the cost of 200 tickets at £9.35 each.

(3) Find the value of 0.9 of £600. (4) What is 150% of 8 ?

(5) What number of 1 cm cubes will fit into a box of volume $\frac{1}{2}$m³ ?

(6) How many quarters in 16 ? (7) 3.4 km + 37 cms

(8) Add the first five even multiples of 7.

(9) How many minutes are there between 11.05 a.m. and 2.02 p.m ?

(10) $8\frac{1}{3} + 2\frac{4}{5}$ (11) $11\frac{1}{7} - 3\frac{3}{4}$

(12) $2\frac{4}{7} \times 2\frac{1}{3}$ (13) $1\frac{13}{15} \div 1\frac{2}{5}$

(14) 9.07 + 13.001 (15) Subtract 2.73 from 6.

(16) 97.43 × 2.4 (17) 36.021 ÷ 0.03

(18) On five successive days a coach driver drove for 6 hours 45 minutes. What was the total time he drove ?

(19) What is the lowest square number greater than 400 ?

(20) Reduce one million and one by sixty three thousand.

Section B

(1) In a group of children two-thirds said they enjoyed playing football and three-quarters said they enjoyed swimming. If 20 of the group said they enjoyed both activities, what was the total number in the group ?

(2) A small fish pond in a garden is rectangular in shape. The sides measure 3 metres by 2 metres and the pond is filled to a depth of 250 cm.

How many litres of water are in the pond ?

(1,000 litres = 1 cubic metre.)

(3) Five girls received an average mark of 45 in an examination. If the marks of four of the girls totalled 211, how many marks did the fifth girl receive ?

(4) The perimeter of a four sided rectangular figure is 84 metres. What is the area of the figure if the length of the rectangle is five times its width ?

(5) When 2.5 is added to a decimal number and the result is multiplied by 3.5 the answer equals 12.95. What is the original decimal number ?

(6) The number of pupils in a school increased by 15% to 414. What was the number of pupils in the school before the increase ?

Section C

(1) When you "dek" two numbers you multiply the larger number by 3 and subtract from the result half of the smaller number.
So, when 5 and 4 are "deked" the result is 13.
This is obtained in the following way:
$5 \times 3 = 15$ and $4 \div 2 = 2$ *and* $15 - 2 = 13$

   (a) What is the result when 6 and 8 are "deked" ?

   (b) When 12 is "deked" with a number the result is 31.
      What is the other number ?

   (c) When a number between 10 and 20 is "deked" with itself, the result is 35. What is the number ?

(2) The following is called an "octal" series because there is an increase of 8 between each number:
$6 - 14 - 22 - 30 - 38$

   (a) What are the next two numbers in the series ?

   (b) If the 48th number in the series is 382, what are the 46th and 47th numbers ? What are the 51st and 52nd numbers ?

   (c) What is the 100th number in the series ?
   (d) What is the 1,000th number in the series ?

(3) A number of pupils at a secondary school were asked whether they enjoyed History, Geography and French. 39 enjoyed History, 43 enjoyed Geography and 47 enjoyed French.
10 said they enjoyed History and Geography, but not French.
4 said they enjoyed History and French, but not Geography.
8 said they enjoyed French and Geography, but not History.
5 said they enjoyed all three subjects.
10 said they disliked all three subjects.

   (a) Put this information onto a Venn diagram.
   (b) How many pupils only liked one subject ?
   (c) How many did not like History ?
   (d) Which was the *least* popular subject ?

(4) The following graph refers to journeys from Manchester to London.
Tom travels from Manchester to London and Mary travels from London to Manchester.

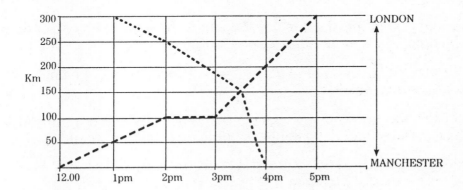

   (a) At what time did Tom stop for a meal and for how long ?
   (b) What was Tom's average speed over the last 200 km of his journey ?
   (c) What time did Mary leave London ?
   (d) At what time and what distance from London did they meet ?
   (e) What was Mary's average speed over the entire journey ?

MODULE EIGHTEEN

Section A

(1) Express one hundred and sixty one thousand four hundred and eighty nine in figures.

(2) How many times can 17 be subtracted from 837 ?

(3) What is the value of the figure underlined: 9$\underline{7}$6,756 ?

(4) $8^{1}/_{3} - 4^{3}/_{4}$

(5) $8^{3}/_{4} + 17^{3}/_{5}$

(6) $4^{3}/_{8} \times 2^{2}/_{7}$

(7) $1^{12}/_{15} \div 3^{3}/_{5}$

(8) $3.7 - 1.051$

(9) 15.3×2.1

(10) $56.013 \div 0.03$

(11) $49.3 + 54.069$

(12) Add 3.6 km and 56 m.

(13) Reduce $8^{3}/_{4}$ to eighths.

(14) How many minutes are there between 11.35 a.m. and 2.15 p.m ?

(15) What is the highest prime number less than 70 ?

(16) How many cm² in 3m² ?

(17) Find the value of $2^{1}/_{2}$% of £3,000.

(18) Is the length of a swimming pool likely to be 5 m, 50 m, 500 m, or 5,000 m ?

(19) Is the weight of a bag of sugar likely to be 100g, 1000g, or 10,000g ?

(20) Add the multiples of 8 between 60 and 81.

Section B

(1) Five men take 12 days digging a trench 40m long, $1^{1}/_{2}$ m wide and 2 m deep. Assuming that all the men work equally hard, how long would it take six men to dig the same trench ?

(2) Joseph was asked to multiply a number by 22, but instead he divided the number by 22. The answer Joseph obtained was 15. What was the correct answer to the question ?

(3) When 5.4 is added to a number and the result is multiplied by 2.1, the final answer is 15.33. What was the original number ?

(4) In a collection for charity, George collected three times more than Henry, but only half as much as Sam. The three boys collected £220 altogether, so how much did they each collect ?

(5) The price of houses increased by 40% between 1986 and 1989.
What was the 1986 value of a house if its value in 1989 was £126,000 ?

(6) At a local football match, one-fifth of the spectators left ten minutes before the end and one-quarter of the remainder left in the last five minutes.
If 900 spectators were in the ground when the final whistle sounded, how many spectators watched the game ?

Section C

(1) A gardener planted seven rose bushes so they formed five lines with three bushes in each line. Show by a diagram how this is possible.
He then planted ten roses in such a way that he had five lines with four rose bushes in each line. In a separate diagram, show how this is possible.

(2) Euler discovered a simple relationship connecting the number of vertices, edges and faces of any three-dimensional shape. This relationship can be stated as $V + F - E = 2$, when V = vertices, E = edges, F = faces.
So in a cube:

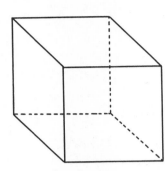

$$V + F - E = 2$$

$$8 + 6 - 12 = 2$$

Write out a similar equation, using the correct numbers for edges, faces and vertices for each of the following shapes:

(a) Tetrahedron   (b) Pyramid   (c) Prism

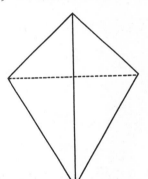   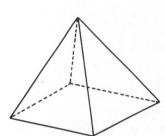   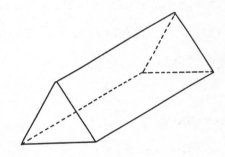

(3) A bookworm ate through five volumes of a series 1-5, starting at volume one, eating through in order to volume five. Each volume was 3 cms thick, including the covers. How many centimetres did the bookworm eat through before it reached the back cover of volume five ?

(4) In a bag there are 27 identical cubes. One of the cubes weighs less than the others. Explain how the lighter cube can be found by using a balance. The most efficient way of discovering this is achieved by using the balance three times.

(5) The Greeks divided numbers into two categories. There were excessive and defective classifications.
An excessive number is defined as a number whose factors, when added together, total less than the original number.
For example 8 is an excessive number because its factors, *excluding* itself, total 7:
$1 + 2 + 4 = 7$.
A defective number is defined as a number whose factors, when added together, total more than the original number.
For example 18 is a defective number because its factors, *excluding* itself, total 21:
$1 + 2 + 3 + 6 + 9$
Classify the numbers between 10 and 20 into these two categories.

MODULE NINETEEN

Section A

(1) How many times does $1^4/_5$ divide into 45 ?

(2) A coach left 37 minutes late at 11.17 a.m. What time should it have left ?

(3) What must be added to 907 to make it exactly divisible by 23 ?

(4) How many quarters are there in $31^3/_4$?   (5) $8^4/_5 + 6^2/_3$

(6) $9.7 \div 1,000$ (7) $2^1/_{10} \div 1^2/_3$

(8) If 1 cm on a map represents 2 km, what does 1 cm^2 represent ?

(9) If $^3/_7$ of a number is 12, what is half the number ?

(10) Add the multiples of 7 between 20 and 50.

(11) Find $7^1/_2\%$ of £160.   (12) $2^5/_8 \times 1^5/_7$

(13) A cube has an edge of 4 cm. What is its volume ?

(14) $18^1/_3 - 13^4/_5$ (15) 39.35×2.7

(16) Find the average of the first five even numbers.

(17) $3.57 \div 1.7$ (18) Find the value of 0.9 of £900.

(19) What is the value of the figure underlined: 9<u>6</u>,743 ?

(20) Find the value of $12^1/_2\%$ of £600.

Section B

(1) Alan lost one ninth of his marbles during morning break. Then at lunch time he lost a quarter of the remainder. This left him with 24 marbles. How many did he start with ?

(2) A slide measures 5 cm in length and 3 cm in width. When put under a microscope the length becomes 30 cm. What is the size of the magnified area ?

(3) Tom, Harry and Fred won £240 in a competition. Tom, who organised the entry, took £80 more than Harry and Fred together. Harry, who posted the coupon, took three times more than Fred. How much did each boy receive ?

(4) Find the total surface area of the net of the oblong box shown in the diagram.

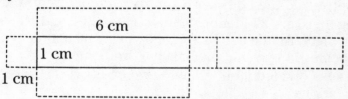

(5) Ann cycles to school in 15 minutes, averaging 24 km/h. When her mother takes her to school by car the journey lasts four minutes.

What is the car's average speed ?

(6) A village church has three bells which chime 24 hours a day. One bell chimes every six minutes, a second bell chimes every 15 minutes and the third bell chimes every 35 minutes. On a particular day, they all chime together at 2.00 p.m.

What would the time be when they next chimed together ?

Section C

(1) The "ESAT" of three numbers is calculated in the following way:

(3, 5, 6) becomes 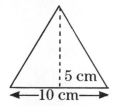 which becomes $\dfrac{43}{30}$

  (a) Work out the "ESAT" of (2, 3, 7).

  (b) If the "ESAT" of $(x, 4, 5)$ works out to $\dfrac{31}{20}$, find the value of x.

  (c) If the "ESAT" of $(4, 3, x)$ works out to $\dfrac{29}{15}$, find the value of x.

(2) To find the area of a triangle you multiply its height by the length of its base, then divide the result by 2.

For example, the area of the following triangle is 25cm²:

5 (height) × 10 (base) = 50 cm²

50 ÷ 2 = 25 cm²

(a) Find the area of the following shapes:

(i) 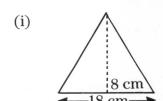   (ii)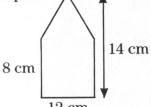

  (b) The area of a triangle is 20cm². If the length of its base is 8 cm., what is the height of the triangle ?

(3) On an Infant School's Sports Day an obstacle race was organised. Six bean bags were placed five metres apart in a straight line. The starting point was ten metres from the first bean bag. The competitors were required to run from the starting point along the line, collect each bean bag, one at a time, and place it at the starting point. Every competitor made six journeys altogether.

  (a) How many metres did each competitor run ?

  (b) How far would a competitor be from the starting point when he was exactly half way through the race ?

(4) A "fractional" tells us how many ways a group of numbers can be arranged.

For example, 1, 2 and 3 can be arranged in six ways, 123, 132, 213, 231, 312 and 321. However, instead of working out all the combinations we can simply write 3 × 2 × 1 = 6.

In the same way four numbers can be arranged in 24 ways: 4 × 3 × 2 × 1 = 24.

  (a) How many different ways can seven figures be arranged ?

  (b) Six children sat on a bench during a P.E. lesson. The teacher told the children to move into as many different seating combinations as possible. If the children could make 12 combinations in one minute, how long would the experiment last ?

MODULE TWENTY

Section A

(1) $976 \times 3{,}212$

(2) Reduce $16^3/_4$ to eighths.

(3) What is the value of the figure underlined: 2,<u>3</u>74,876 ?

(4) Find the value of 0.3 of 260.

(5) Express 0.75m^3 in cm^3.

(6) Find the cost of 300 books at £3.95 each.

(7) How many minutes between 4.15 p.m. and 9.05 p.m ?

(8) If the date is 30th March, what will the date be in 100 days time ?

(9) $6^1/_3 - 3^4/_5$

(10) $5^1/_7 \times 2^1/_3$

(11) $15^4/_5 + 3^3/_4$

(12) $11^1/_{34} \div 1^{12}/_{13}$

(13) $5.7 - 3.149$

(14) $9.6 + 0.96 + 0.096$

(15) 37.6×2.5

(16) $18.021 \div 0.03$

(17) A man walking due north turned an angle of 45 degrees to his right. What was his new direction ?

(18) 8 hours 47 mins $\times$ 6

(19) Express $37^1/_2\%$ as a fraction.

(20) Add the odd multiples of 3 between 12 and 25.

Section B

(1) What is the lowest number 33, 35 and 55 will divide into without leaving a remainder ?

(2) The cost of 13 apples was £1.31. Find the cost of 65 apples, assuming that all the apples were the same price.

(3) A journey was covered at an average speed of 80 km/h in $4^1/_2$ hours.
How long would the same journey take at an average speed of 60 km/h ?

(4) A mixed number is added to $2^3/_4$. The result is then divided by $1^1/_4$. The final answer is 5.
What is the mixed number ?

(5) For every two first class stamps priced 20p each, John bought three second class stamps priced 15p.
If he spent £12.75, how many stamps did he buy ?

(6) In a random sample of top business men, it was found that 20 had a British made car and 40 had a Japanese or European car.
If 48 men were questioned, how many had just a British made car ?

Section C

1. Set A is a set of numbers which are multiples of 7, between 6 and 100.
   Set B is a set of numbers which are divisible by 4, between 6 and 100.
   Set C is a set of numbers which are divisible by 5, between 6 and 100.
   (a) How many elements in A∩B ?
   (b) How many elements in (A∩B)∪C?
   (c) How many elements in B∩C ?

(2) A *plane* shape is the correct name for a flat shape: it has three or more sides but no depth. A three-dimensional or *solid* shape, on the other hand, does have depth.
   Which of the following shapes appear to be plane, and which solid:

   (a)   (b) 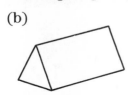   (c) 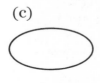   (d) 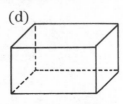   (e)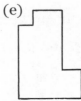

   Now state which of the following named shapes are plane, and which solid:
   (f) a cube   (g) a circle   (h) a triangle   (i) a pyramid   (j) a sphere

(3) A plane shape is said to have a line or axis of symmetry if, by folding the shape along the line, one half of it will fit exactly over the other half.
   In the following example the shape has two lines of symmetry.
   If it is folded along the first one, area A will fit over area B, and if folded on the second, area C will fit over area D.

   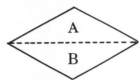   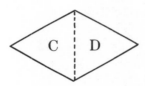

   Draw each of the following shapes and put in *all* axes of symmetry.

       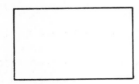   

(4) The way a fruit machine works is that once four balls enter column A, the column empties and one ball enters column B. When four balls are in column B, the column empties and one ball enters column C and so to column D.

   D   C   B   A

   (a) Calculate the number of balls that have entered column A to achieve the following situations.

   (i)   D   C   B   A   (ii)   D   C   B   A

   (b) When column D is full, the column empties and £50 is paid out. How much profit is made by the machine if each ball entering column A averages a 30p stake ?

43

MODULE TWENTY-ONE

Section A

(1) $7 \div 1,000$

(2) How many fifths in 25 ?

(3) 3.3 km + 3 km 30 cm.

(4) 4.6 m − 3 cm.

(5) What must be added to 601 to make it exactly divisible by 17 ?

(6) £17.45 × 9

(7) 8 hours 25 mins ÷ 5

(8) 674 × 213

(9) 6.7 + 15.007

(10) 6.1 − 2.097

(11) 94.87 × 2.5

(12) 15.021 ÷ 0.003

(13) $8^4/_5 + 6^2/_3$

(14) $15^1/_4 - 3^4/_7$

(15) $7^3/_5 \times 8^3/_4$

(16) What are the prime numbers between 50 and 60 ?

(17) What is the total length of the edges of a cube whose volume is 8cm³ ?

(18) In the number 87,643, put in a decimal point to make the 6 into $^6/_{10}$.

(19) What is the date 90 days after 31st July ?

(20) $9^1/_3 \div 5^5/_6$

Section B

(1) A member of Hale Cycling Club covered the 80 km to the coast in three hours but, due to a high wind, only averaged 16 km/h on the return journey.
What was the average speed of the total journey ?

(2) In two successive spelling tests, Robert scored 18 out of a possible 20, and 23 out of a possible 25. Which was the better performance ?

(3) On a hike, a boy's father covered in two strides the distance the boy covered in three strides. The father's stride was 90 cms.
How many strides did the boy take on a walk of $13^1/_2$ km ?

(4) A map is drawn to a scale of 2 cm : 1 km. A parkland area on the map is represented by an area of four square centimetres. What is the actual area of the parkland ?

(5) In a group, half had visited the theatre in the previous month, whereas three quarters of the group had visited the cinema. If 40 had visited both, how many had only been to the cinema ?

(6) After four games a first division football team's average attendance was 38,500. What would the attendance in the fifth game need to be if the average for the five games was to be 40,000 ?

Section C

(1) A pupil was asked to carry out a survey on whether visitors to a restaurant drank coffee or tea after their meal. The pupil presented her answers in the following Venn diagram:

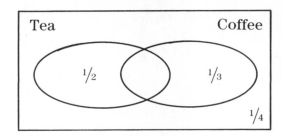

If seven customers had both tea and coffee, how many customers did she question ?

(2) The "kae" of a number is the sum of its digits. It is indicated by the letter K.
For example, K4610 = 11 because $4 + 6 + 1 + 0 = 11$.
The double "kae" of a number is the sum of the digits of the answer of the "kae" of the number. For example:
KK4610 = 2 because $4 + 6 + 1 + 0 = 11$ *and* $1 + 1 = 2$.

(a) Work out K946
(b) Work out KK495
(c) x is a number between 10 and 150. What is the greatest value of Kx ?
(d) x stands for a number between 210 and 220. If its "kae" value is 7, what number does x stand for ?

(3) The "goras" of two numbers is calculated in the following example: The "goras" of 6 and 8 is 10 because $6 \times 6 + 8 \times 8 = 36 + 64 = 100$ and $10 \times 10 = 100$.

(a) What is the "goras" of 12 and 5 ?
(b) The "goras" of two numbers is 5. If one of the numbers is 3, what is the second number ?

(4) In one hour a number of passengers were questioned as to their destination as they went through Passport Control at Manchester Airport. Their replies are represented in the following pie chart, which has been divided into equal sections by the marks shown around its edge.

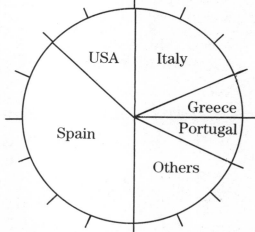

Given the additional information that 400 passengers were destined for the U.S.A., illustrate the information provided in either a block or line graph of your own using the following axes:

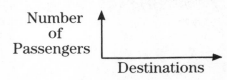

MODULE TWENTY-TWO

Section A

(1) Express in figures: five hundred and six thousand two hundred and ninety seven.

(2) Put into words: 371,036

(3) $8^3/_5 + 16^7/_8$

(4) $9^1/_7 - 3^3/_4$

(5) $2^7/_{10} \times 1^2/_3$

(6) $4^1/_8 \div 2^3/_4$

(7) $19.07 + 161.031$

(8) 91.7×2.1

(9) $3.6 - 1.097$

(10) $1512 \div 0.02$

(11) The cost of 14 books is £77. What is the cost of each book ?

(12) How many times can 17 be taken from 1017 ?

(13) What is 1845 hours in 12 hour clock time ?

(14) How many fifths in $5^1/_5$?

(15) Today is Wednesday 16th April. What will the day and date be in 80 days time ?

(16) Five consecutive numbers have an average of 17. What is the smallest of the numbers ?

(17) 3.4 km $+ 56$ m

(18) What are the prime factors of 36 ?

(19) How many different three digit numbers can be made from the digits 8, 9 and 5, using each digit only once ?

(20) On a scale of 1 cm: 4 km, what area does 4 cm² represent ?

Section B

(1) A netball team averaged 9 points a game for the first five games of the season. After the sixth game this average had been increased to 10 points.
How many points were scored in the sixth game ?

(2) After two years Mr. Smith discovered that the value of his car had fallen by 40%. If his car was then valued at £6,900 what was the original value of the car ?

(3) A slide measures 6 cm by 4 cm. When it is projected onto a screen its length is 1.2 m. What is the area of the projected slide ?

(4) A farmer estimated he had sufficient fodder to feed his 50 cows for 40 days. The same day he sold 30 cows. How long would the fodder last the remaining cows ?

(5) A coach driver on a nine day tour drove for 7 hours 45 mins a day. How many hours did he drive for altogether on the tour ?

(6) When 1.7 is added to a number and the result is divided by 0.3, the result is 15.
What was the original number ?

Section C

(1) To "Buxton" two numbers the first number is squared and the second number is subtracted from the result. The symbol (B) means to "Buxton". For example (B) 3 and 2 equals 7 because $3 \times 3 = 9$ and $9 - 2 = 7$.

    (a) Calculate (B) 8 and 5
    (b) Calculate (B) 7 and 7
    (c) What is the value of x, when (B) x and 9 equals 40 ?
    (d) What is the value of x, when (B) x and x equals 90 ?
    (e) Study the following pattern and write in the next two lines:
        (B) 1 and 1 = 0
        (B) 2 and 4 = 0
        (B) 3 and 9 = 0
        (B) 4 and 16 = 0

(2) Brian discovered that the sum of the first three odd numbers equalled 9, that is $1 + 3 + 5 = 9$. An alternative way of making the same calculation was $3 \times 3 = 9$.
In the same way the first six odd numbers totalled 36 when added together: $1 + 3 + 5 + 7 + 9 + 11 = 36$. An alternative way of making the calculation was $6 \times 6 = 36$.
    (a) Calculate the sum of the first ten odd numbers.
    (b) Work out the sum of the odd numbers 1 to 69 inclusive.
    (c) If the sum of the consecutive odd numbers starting at 1 is 900, what is the greatest odd number in the series ?

(3) When four numbers are put into a rectangle, a "number one" calculation is worked out. This can be shown in the following calculation:

$$\begin{array}{|cc|} \hline 8 & 4 \\ 6 & 5 \\ \hline \end{array} = (8 \times 5) - (6 \times 4) = 40 - 24 = 16$$

    (a) Work out:
$$\begin{array}{|cc|} \hline 7 & 3 \\ 5 & 8 \\ \hline \end{array}$$

    (b) What is the missing number when the following "number one" calculation results in 9 ?
$$\begin{array}{|cc|} \hline 9 & 15 \\ 6 & x \\ \hline \end{array}$$

    (c) In the following "number one" calculation x represents two missing numbers and y represents two missing numbers. If the result of the calculation is 56, what are the values of x and y ?
$$\begin{array}{|cc|} \hline x & y \\ y & x \\ \hline \end{array}$$

(4) A display box containing nine Mars Bars weighs 730 g. After the sale of four Mars Bars, the total weight of the display box and remaining Mars Bars is 450g. If the display box holds 20 Mars Bars, what is its total weight when full ?

MODULE TWENTY-THREE

Section A

(1) Increase five thousand and seven by sixty one thousand seven hundred and ninety seven.

(2) Find the cost of 17 theatre tickets priced £8.75 each.

(3) A school starts at 9.15 a.m. and finishes at 4.04 p.m. How long are the children in school ?

(4) $8\frac{1}{3} - 2\frac{4}{5}$

(5) $5\frac{1}{4} \times 2\frac{2}{3}$

(6) $1\frac{11}{16} \div 2\frac{1}{4}$

(7) $97.674 + 9.09$

(8) $3.7 - 1.097$

(9) 97.6×0.002

(10) $1.02 \div 0.17$

(11) $8\frac{3}{4} + 2\frac{2}{5}$

(12) 7 hours 15 mins − 2 hours 39 mins

(13) 27 hours 24 mins ÷ 6

(14) 6 hours 39 mins + 2 hours 43 mins

(15) 7 hours 39 mins × 7

(17) What is the value of 7 in 43.097 ?

(18) 5.6 m + 42 cm

(19) What is $\frac{3}{4}$ of $\frac{7}{8}$ of 64 ?

(20) How many quarters in $17\frac{1}{2}$?

Section B

(1) Josh leaves home at 8.40 a.m. and arrives at school at 8.55 a.m. His average speed of walking is 6 km/h and he walks home each day at the same average speed.
How far does he walk in a week when he attends school on five occasions ?

(2) What is the lowest number 15, 21 and 33 can all be divided into without leaving a remainder ?

(3) A group organiser realised he could completely fill a number of 21 seater or 33 seater coaches with his group. What is the smallest number of people in his group ?

(4) Find the total cost of ten books priced £2.95 each, nine books priced £11.35 for three and seven books whose average cost is £6.50.

(5) Georgina was told to add seventy four thousand six hundred and nine to a certain number, instead she subtracted. Georgina's answer was four thousand and ninety seven. What should her answer have been ?

(6) Seven girls obtained an average score of 64% in their maths exam and three boys obtained an average score of 59%. What was the average score of the group ?

Section C

(1) A rectangular shaped tray measuring 20 cm by 24 cm is used to hold mini-snooker balls. Balls of various sizes are put into the tray.

    (a) How many balls of diameter $1\frac{1}{2}$ cm will fit into the tray ?

    (b) How many balls of diameter $2\frac{1}{2}$ cm will fit into the tray ?

    (c) A number of balls are placed in the tray. If there are 30 balls in the tray, what is the diameter of each ball ?

    (d) A number of balls are left in the tray. Black balls with a value of 7 points, pink with a value of 6 points, green with a value of 3 points and red, with a value of 1 point. A player picks up six balls and finds the total value of the points to be 26. What are the colours of the balls he has picked out?

(2) Numbers can form different patterns, for example:

  Six can form a rectangular pattern   Nine can form a square pattern

    (a) What is the lowest number that can form both a rectangular and square shape ?

    (b) How many different rectangular and square patterns can 64 make ?

    (c) If two square pattern numbers are added together, does a square pattern number always result ?

    (d) If a square pattern number and a rectangular pattern number are added together, does a rectangular pattern number always result ?

(3) The following graph represents part of a motorway route across the Alps.

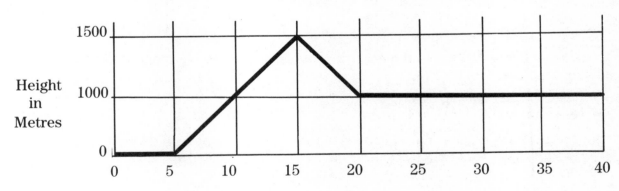

Mr Steel drove over this route on his way to a skiing holiday and travelled the same route on his return. He checked his speed and discovered that on the flat he averaged 60 km/h. He averaged 30 km/h going uphill and 75 km/h going downhill.

What was the difference in time travelling from A to B, compared with travelling back from B to A ?

MODULE TWENTY-FOUR

Section A

(1) Increase six hundred and ninety nine thousand nine hundred and seventy four by sixteen thousand and seventy four.

(2) Reduce 97 by $\frac{3}{4}$ of 64.

(3) $17 \div 1,000$

(4) $5\frac{2}{3} + 11\frac{4}{5}$

(5) $8\frac{1}{3} - 4\frac{3}{5}$

(6) $4\frac{3}{8} \times 3\frac{1}{5}$

(7) $3\frac{1}{9} \div 4\frac{2}{3}$

(8) $93.748 + 9.476$

(9) $3.7 - 1.907$

(10) 97.35×2.7

(11) $5.95 \div 0.17$

(12) How many minutes are there between 11.35 a.m. and 3.15 p.m ?

(13) Add the multiples of three between 80 and 95.

(14) Find the cost of 50 stamps at 15p each.

(15) Find the surface area of a cube of edge 7 cm.

(16) What is the value of 0.3 of £6,000 ?

(17) What is the value of $12\frac{1}{2}$% of £240 ?

(18) 3.4 km + 85 m

(19) Express 973,487 to the nearest thousand.

(20) How many cm³ in $\frac{1}{4}$ m³ ?

Section B

(1) Calculate the area of the following shape:

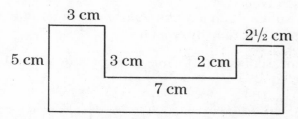

(2) Mrs Warner drove 160 km to the coast in 3 hours 12 minutes and made the return journey at an average speed of 30 km/h.

(a) What was her average speed to the coast ?
(b) How long did the return journey take ?

(3) Two brothers shared the firm's profits in a ratio of how many cars they sold. Christopher sold five cars for every four sold by Peter. The firm made £63,000 profit last year. How much did Peter earn ?

(4) When 5.2 is added to a number and the result is multiplied by 22, the final answer is 17.38. What was the original number ?

(5) A container 8 m by 4 m by 2 m is $\frac{7}{8}$ full. How many boxes measuring 1 m by 75 cm by 50 cm could still be placed in the container ?

(6) A photograph measuring 6 cm by 12 cm is enlarged so that its enlarged area is 648 cm². What are the measurements of the enlargement ?

50

Section C

(1) A running track on a school's games field is made up of two half-circular ends and two straight sections:-

radius

The radius of each end is 28 metres. The distance round each half circular end is found by dividing the radius by 7 and multiplying the result by 22. The total distance round the track is 400 metres.
How long is each straight section of the track ?

(2) When the letter S is written in front of another number, it means multiply that number by itself.

For example, S4 = 16   That is 4 × 4 = 16
          S9 = 91   That is 9 × 9 = 81

(a) Calculate the values of (i) S55   (ii) S513

In the same way A before a number means add 1 to the number.
For example, A8 = 9   that is 8 + 1 = 9
In the same way B before a number means subtract 1 from the number.
For example, B10 = 9   That is 10 − 1 = 9

(b) Calculate the values of (i) B15   (ii) A19

When two or more letters are placed before a number, the process carried out first is dictated by the letter *nearest the number*.
For example, BS5
          First, S5 = 5 × 5 = 25
          Then, B25 = 25 − 1 = 24

(c) Calculate the value BS7
(d) Find the values of (i) AS3   (ii) BS3   (iii) BSS3
(e) Find the value of AS3 × BS3. What do you notice ?

(3) The following two sums have been carried out in Base Four.
Fill in the missing numbers.

(a)
```
  1  a  2
  1  3  3  +
 ─────────
  3  2  6
```

(b)
```
        2  1  3
           3  x
  ───────────────
  1  y  1  1  0
     1  0  3  2
  ───────────────
  2  z  2  0  2
```

(4) James bought a cheap calculator which only displayed six digits. When he added 2 to 999,999 it displayed 000,001. When he multiplied 999,999 by 2, it displayed 999,998.

(a) If he added 90 to 999,990, what would be displayed ?
(b) If he multiplied 987,654 by 3, what would be displayed ?
(c) When he added 900,000 to a number it displayed 600,000. What was the number ?

MODULE TWENTY-FIVE

Section A

(1) $97,492 + 6,983 + 5,462 + 987$

(2) $97,001 - 3,896$

(3) 978×432

(4) $976 \div 17$

(5) $15^3/_4 + 6^2/_3$

(6) Express $^3/_4$ as a percentage.

(7) $6^2/_3 \times 10^1/_2$

(8) $6^1/_4 \div 1^7/_8$

(9) $3.7 + 15.003$

(10) $9.3 - 6.031$

(11) $37.1 - 2.003$

(12) 37.54×2.4

(13) $15.0111 \div 0.003$

(14) 9 hours 37 mins + 6 hours 39 mins

(15) 11 hours 15 mins − 2 hours 38 mins

(16) 9 hours 39 mins × 9

(17) 24 hours 15 mins ÷ 5

(18) 8.7 km + 3 km 425 m

(19) 8 litres 39 ml − 3 litres 98 ml

(20) How many grams in 4.3 kg ?

Section B

(1) Mr. Orford left home and arrived at his office ten minutes later at 8.45 a.m. If he cycled at an average speed of 24 km/h., what is the distance between his home and his office ?

(2) Rachel was given one free sticker for every six stickers she bought. She finally ended up with 161 stickers. How many of these stickers did she actually buy ?

(3) The perimeter of the following rectangle is 400 cm. By first finding the value of x, find the area of the rectangle.

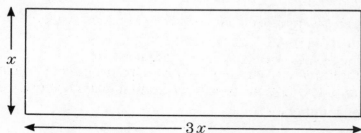

(4) A number of passengers were questioned at Glasgow Airport. 65% of those questioned had flown to Europe in the previous year and 55% had flown to America in the same period. If 400 passengers had flown to both Europe and America, how many were questioned ?

(5) Over a period of seven days, the sun shone for an average of 9 hours a day. Over the first six days, the average amount of sunshine was $8^1/_2$ hours a day. What was the amount of sunshine on the seventh day ?

(6) In a giant box of Smarties, it was found that the number of Smarties in the box could be divided equally amongst 5, 7 or 11 children without any Smarties being left over. If there is a guarantee that there are more than 1,000 Smarties in the box, what is the lowest number of Smarties that could be in the box ?

Section C

(1) 32 is said to be a "trunk" number because at the end of the "trunking" process, the number is 1. The process of "trunking" can be shown in the following example:

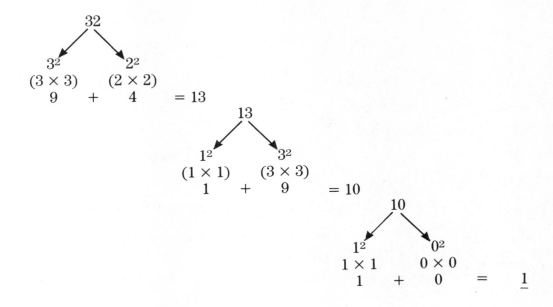

(a) is 23 a "trunk" number ?
(b) is 31 a "trunk" number ?
(c) is 64 a "trunk" number ?

(2) The number 15 can be expressed as a sum of consecutive numbers in two ways:

$$7 + 8 = 15$$
$$4 + 5 + 6 = 15$$

The number 45 can be expressed as the sum of consecutive numbers in five ways. What are these ?

(3) Certain two digit numbers when they go through a process of "separate and square" always have a final result of 0. Study the following example which shows that 49 is one such number.

$$49 \rightarrow 9^2 - 4^2 = 81 - 16 = 65$$
$$65 \rightarrow 6^2 - 5^2 = 36 - 25 = 11$$
$$11 \rightarrow 1^2 - 1^2 = 1 - 1 = 0$$

Find another number which results in 0 in the same manner.

(4) Show, by using three of your own examples, which of the following mathematical statements are always correct.

(a) All odd numbers, except one, can be expressed as the sum of *two* consecutive numbers.

(b) All the multiples of five, except five, can be expressed as the sum of five consecutive numbers.

MODULE TWENTY-SIX

Section A

(1) Reduce twenty thousand and ten by six thousand nine hundred and eight.

(2) $11\frac{1}{3} - 9\frac{3}{4}$

(3) $3\frac{4}{7} \times 2\frac{1}{5}$

(4) $4\frac{8}{9} \div 3\frac{2}{3}$

(5) 39.3×2.7

(6) $15.05 \div 0.7$

(7) $6 \div 1,000$

(8) Express 0.55 as a fraction in its lowest terms.

(9) How many minutes are there in 3.2 hours ?

(10) What is the value of the digit underlined: 53.67<u>4</u> ?

(11) 679×359

(12) 7 kg 7 g − 2.7 kg

(13) 9 hours 38 mins × 7

(14) 3.7 m + 69 cm

(15) $9 + 0.9 + 0.99 + 0.999$

(16) Find the value of 0.9 of £890.

(17) What is the value of $37\frac{1}{2}\%$ of 16?

(18) Find the lowest number which 3, 6 and 7 will all divide into.

(19) Ten posts in a straight line are 1m apart. What is the total length of the line given that each post is 25 cm wide ?

(20) How many litres of water will a cube of edge 2 m hold ?

Section B

(1) The sum of two numbers is 48. The difference between the numbers is 14. What are the two numbers?

(2) A carpet measuring 4 m by 5 m leaves a margin of 1 m when placed in a bedroom. What area of the bedroom is not covered by the carpet ?

(3) A shop front is painted red, green and white. If half is painted red, one-fifth green and 9 metres white, what is the length of the shop front ?

(4) John leaves home at 8.40 a.m. and arrives at school at 8.55 a.m. If he cycles at an average speed of 22 km/h., how far from school does he live ?

(5) When 1.5 is added to a number and the result is multiplied by 1.2 the answer is 6. What is the original number ?

(6) Find the total length of the edges of the following cuboid:

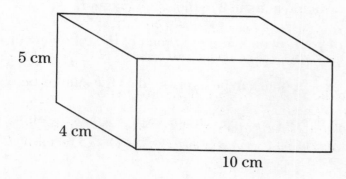

5 cm

4 cm

10 cm

54

Section C

(1) In a triangle, where one of the angles is 90 degrees, it is possible to calculate the length of the longest side of the triangle if you know the length of the remaining two sides.
The side is calculated in the following way:

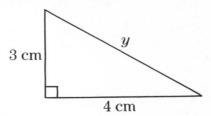

$$(4 \times 4) + (3 \times 3) = (y \times y)$$
$$(16) \quad + (9) \quad = (y \times y)$$
$$25 \quad = (y \times y)$$
$$5 \quad = y$$

Using the same method, calculate the length of P and Q in the following right-angled triangles:

(a)

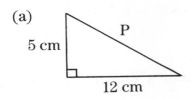

(b)

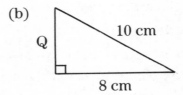

(2) A farmer had 200 metres of fencing. He wished to enclose part of a field for his bull and wanted to arrange the fencing in such a way so as to enclose the largest possible rectangular area. How would he do this ?

(3) A "dube" is a pair of numbers written in brackets, so (2,5) is a "dube". Two "dubes" can be "junced" as in the following example:
(2,5) "junced" with (3,7) becomes $(2 \times 7 + 5 \times 3, 5 \times 7) = (29,35)$.
All "dubes" can be cancelled in the same way as fractions, so (8,6) can be written (4,3) with both numbers being divided by 2.
   (a) Work out (1,4) "junced" with (3,7)
   (b) Write in its simplest form (90,45)
   (c) Find x in (x,11) "junced" with (x,9) = (80,99)
   (d) Find x in (x,6) "junced" with (x,7) = (13,14)

(4) In the game of Hull darts there are two colours on the board. A dart that lands on a red colour scores 5 points; a dart that lands on a blue colour scores 8 points. The points are then added together to give a total score. Whilst it is possible to score 18 (two red and one blue), it is impossible to score 17.
   (a) Bill scored 40 points. How could he have done this ?
   (b) Alan scored 53 points. How could he have done this ?
   (c) Write down the impossible scores between 20 and 30.

(5) A worker in a toy factory was paid a basic £80 a week plus £1.25 for every doll he made over 70 dolls a week.
   (a) In one week he made 79 dolls. How much did he earn ?
   (b) How many toys did he make in a week when he earned £117.50 ?
   (c) In one year when he worked for 48 weeks, it was discovered he had made 4,080 dolls. Assuming he was paid £80 for 52 weeks, how much did he earn altogether ?

MODULE TWENTY-SEVEN

Section A

(1) $8,796 \times 89$

(2) $879 \div 19$

(3) $8^4/_7 + 5^3/_4$

(4) $10^1/_7 - 5^3/_4$

(5) $4^9/_{10} \times 2^1/_7$

(6) $5^1/_3 \div 2^2/_3$

(7) $37.06 + 936.009$

(8) 843×9.7

(9) $9 \div 0.003$

(10) $4^2/_3 \div 3^1/_9$

(11) How many numbers, including 1 and 40, divide into 40 ?

(12) If 1 litre equals 1,000 cm³, add 3.4 litres and 202 cm³. Give your answer in cm³.

(13) How many cm in 532 mm ?

(14) 35 hours 24 mins ÷ 6

(15) A cube has a volume of 27 m³. Find its total surface area.

(16) If today is Thursday 15th June, what will the day and date be in 60 days time ?

(17) Find 0.4 of £360.

(18) Express $7^1/_2$% as a fraction in its lowest terms.

(19) Express three hundred and eighty one thousand seven hundred and sixty five in figures.

(20) Add the prime numbers between 35 and 45.

Section B

(1) Paul discovered that for every two pence coin he possessed, he had two twenty pence piece coins. He had 33 coins altogether. How much money did he have ?

(2) A joiner measured a piece of wood and took it to be 6.6 m long. He found later that he had incorrectly measured the wood and that it was 20% shorter. How long was the piece of wood ?

(3) A businessman flew from Manchester to Munich in $2^1/_4$ hours. The average speed of the flight was 600 km/h. What is the distance between Manchester and Munich ?

(4) $2^1/_4$ is added to a mixed number. The number is then multiplied by $1^1/_3$. The answer is $7^2/_3$. What was the original mixed number ?

(5) Chris remembers that a friend's telephone number is the first number that can be divided by his friend's age, his uncle's age and an aunt's age. If the three ages are 12, 40 and 44, what is the telephone number ?

(6) A shopkeeper allows a 5% reduction for immediate payment. A customer pays £76.00 cash. What was the original price ?

Section C

(1) There are only 17 perfect numbers. A perfect number is defined as a number which is equal to the sum of all the numbers that divide into it exactly. 6 is a perfect number because the numbers that divide into it add up to 6, that is $1 + 2 + 3 = 6$. The next perfect number lies between 20 and 30. What is this number?

(2) There are four cages in a row. At one end two cages are occupied by two monkeys, whilst at the other end the cages are occupied by two apes.

M	M	A	A

The zoo-keeper decides to swap the cages so that the two monkeys finish up in the cages occupied by the two apes and the apes finish up in the cages once occupied by the monkeys.

The keeper can only move two animals at a time and then only into adjoining cages. Obviously he cannot leave two animals in the same cage. What is the least number of moves the zoo-keeper can make?

(3) A line of symmetry, sometimes called an axis of symmetry, divides a shape in half so that one half is a perfect reflection of the other. A number of shapes or figures have more than one axis of symmetry, for example, a rectangle, whilst other shapes have none.

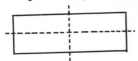

A rectangle – two axes of symmetry

One axis of symmetry

No axes of symmetry

In each of the following put in the axes of symmetry.

(a)   (b)   (c)   (d)   (e)   (f)   (g)

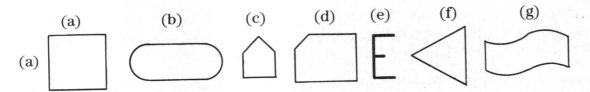

(4) Jenny thought of a number between 1 and 10. She discovered that half of the number was exactly one more than one-third of it. What was the number she first thought of?

(5) Juan was sheltering from the sun under the tallest palm tree in the village. He decided to compare the length of the tree's shadow with its actual height, which he knew to be 28 metres. He measured the shadow and discovered it to be 21 metres.

   (a) How tall was Juan if his shadow was 1.2 m?
   (b) Juan's friend, Pedro, was 1.84 m tall. How long was his shadow?
   (c) The two boys measured the length of the shadow of Juan's house and found it to be 12 metres. What was the height of the house?

MODULE TWENTY-EIGHT

Section A

(1) Express in figures three hundred and six thousand, four hundred and ninety seven.

(2) $16^3/_4 - 5^7/_9$

(3) $2^1/_7 \times 1^3/_5$

(4) $3^1/_9 \div 2^1/_3$

(5) $11^3/_4 + 2^2/_5$

(6) 39.3×2.2

(7) $15.05 + 0.7$

(8) $15.05 \div 0.7$

(9) $6 \div 100$

(10) Express $2^1/_2\%$ as a fraction

(11) How many minutes are there in $3^2/_5$ hours ?

(12) Put a decimal point in 38764 to give 7 the value of $^7/_{10}$.

(13) 976×834

(14) 7 kg 7 g − 2.7 kg

(15) How many minutes between 11.15 a.m. and 3.05 p.m ?

(16) How many 5 pence coins are required to make up £3.25 ?

(17) Add the prime numbers between 25 and 35.

(18) Find the value of 0.3 of £40.

(19) How many eighths in 64 ?

(20) Express 2.4 km in cm.

Section B

(1) The members of a class were asked to state which colour they preferred from red, white and blue. Only one colour could be chosen by each person. Half preferred blue; a fifth preferred red; and nine people preferred white. How many pupils were in the class ?

(2) When 1.5 is added to a number and the result is multiplied by 1.2, the answer is 6. What is the original number ?

(3) A centre-forward scored three times as many goals as the next highest scorer. If they scored 36 goals between them, how many did the centre-forward score ?

(4) A coat priced at £80 was reduced by 15% in a sale. What was the sale price of the coat ?

(5) A girl cycled for three hours at an average speed of 12 km/h. Then she cycled for a further two hours at an average speed of 17 km/h.
   (a) What distance did she cover ?
   (b) What was her average speed throughout the journey ?

(6) What is the lowest three digit number which when divided by 5, 6 and 12 leaves a remainder of 4 ?

Section C

(1) The symbol ☐ stands for the greatest *whole* number not larger than the number in the rectangle.

So,

$$\boxed{6^{1}/_{4}} = 6 \quad \text{and} \quad \boxed{7^{3}/_{4}} = 7$$

Calculate the following:

(a) $\boxed{15^{1}/_{4}}$ divided by 3

(b) $\boxed{21^{3}/_{5}}$ divided by $\boxed{7^{4}/_{5}}$

(c) $\boxed{7^{1}/_{2}}$ divided by $\boxed{2^{1}/_{2}}$

(2) When you spin the wheel below, the chance of it stopping when the number 2 is opposite the arrow is one-in-eight, written as $^{1}/_{8}$.

This is because there are *eight* numbers altogether and only *one* 2. This chance is called "probability"

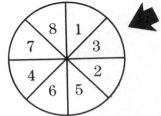

(a) What is the probability of 7 stopping opposite the arrow ?
(b) What is the probability of a prime number stopping opposite the arrow ?
(c) What is the probability of a square number stopping there ?
(d) What is the probability of an even number stopping there ?

(3) In the set of numbers 9, 14, 19, 24, each number is five more than the number before it.

(a) Give the next three numbers.

(b) The 15th number in the series is 79. What are the 13th and 18th numbers ?

(c) The 80th number in the series is 404. What are the 82nd and 78th numbers ?

(d) What are the 43rd and 97th numbers in the series ?

(4) Thomas bought a magazine for 39p. He paid for this with a 50 pence coin. In how many different ways could he have received his change ?

(5) Study the following number pattern:

$143 \times 2 \times 7 = 2{,}002$
$143 \times 3 \times 7 = 3{,}003$
$143 \times 4 \times 7 = 4{,}004$
$143 \times 5 \times 7 = 5{,}005$
$143 \times 6 \times 7 = 6{,}006$
$143 \times 7 \times 7 = 7{,}007$

(a) Complete the next line.
(b) Can you give an explanation for the pattern of answers ?

MODULE TWENTY-NINE

Section A

(1) Express in figures seven hundred and six thousand four hundred and one.

(2) Reduce twelve thousand and one by ninety nine.

(3) What must be added to seven thousand and one to make it exactly divisible by 19 ?

(4) Divide 19 by 1,000.

(5) $9^4/_5 + 6^1/_3$

(6) Find the cost of 100 tickets at £9.57 each.

(7) $10^1/_3 - 2^4/_7$

(8) $2^1/_{10} \times 1^2/_3$

(9) $6^1/_8 \div 1^3/_4$

(10) $3.7 + 1.008$

(11) $8.1 - 2.009$

(12) 3.1×2.05

(13) $3.2 \div 0.016$

(14) Express 14% as a fraction.

(15) Express 0.03 as a fraction.

(16) Reduce $4^1/_2$ to quarters.

(17) Add the odd numbers between 81 and 89.

(18) $3.2 \text{ kg} + 85 \text{ g}$

(19) Today is Tuesday 13th March. What will the day and date be in 90 days time ?

(20) What is a number when $^7/_5$ of that number equals 21 ?

Section B

(1) A piece of paper measures 32 cm by 20 cm. What is its area ?
A margin of 1 cm is cut off all the way round. What area remains ?

(2) A container measures 3 m by 4 m by 75 cm. If 1,000 cm^3 = 1 litre, how many litres of water does the container hold ?

(3) After four homeworks, Bernard found that his average mark was 9. In his fifth homework he did considerably better and increased his average to 10. What mark did he achieve in his fifth homework ?

(4) A spot check was carried out in a school of 160 pupils and it was discovered that $12^1/_2$% were not wearing a school tie. How many pupils *were* wearing school ties ?

(5) Isaac cycled a distance of 40 km in 2 hours 30 minutes. What was his average speed expressed in km/h ?

(6) In a group of 80 people, 47 enjoyed tea, 31 enjoyed coffee and 12 disliked both tea and coffee. How many in the group liked only one drink ?

Section C

(1) If four points are marked on the circumference of a circle, it is only possible to draw four lines connecting the points without forming a triangle.

   (a) How many lines could be joined connecting six dots on the circumference of a circle without forming a triangle ?

   (b) How many lines could be joined connecting eight dots on the circumference of a circle without forming a triangle ?

(2) In a town there are only six streets. All the streets are straight. It was decided to put one set of traffic lights at each road intersection. What is the greatest number of sets of traffic lights that might be needed ?

(3) In the sum

$$\begin{array}{c c c c} F & O & U & R \\ & O & N & E \\ \hline F & I & V & E \end{array}$$

each letter represents a number.
Replace the letters with the numbers to obtain the correct sum.

(4) Three coins are placed on a table with heads uppermost. A "move" consists of turning over *two* coins at a time. Is it possible to have all tails uppermost ? If so, how many "moves" are required ?

(5) A number such as 231 is referred to as a "hale" prime number because as you remove each digit from the left you are left with a prime number:
231 = prime number; 31 = prime number; 2 = prime number.

A number such as 373 is referred to as a "prep" number because as you remove each digit from the right you are left with a prime number:
373 = prime number; 37 = prime number; 3 = prime number.

   (a) State two "hale" prime numbers.
   (b) Give two "prep" numbers.

MODULE THIRTY

Section A

(1) Express three hundred and ten thousand and ten in figures.

(2) 976×35

(3) $18\frac{2}{3} + 4\frac{3}{4}$

(4) $9\frac{1}{3} - 4\frac{2}{5}$

(5) $2\frac{6}{7} \times 1\frac{2}{5}$

(6) $3\frac{1}{8} \div 7\frac{1}{2}$

(7) $9.47 + 5.876$

(8) $3.1 - 0.001$

(9) 15.4×2.7

(10) $5.4 \div 0.02$

(11) £36.74 + 376 pence

(12) 3 km. 402 m + 13.4 km

(13) How many quarters in $18\frac{3}{4}$?

(14) 18 hours 35 mins ÷ 5

(15) Add the prime numbers between 18 and 30.

(16) What is the value of the digit underlined: 375.4<u>7</u>8 ?

(17) How many minutes between 11.13 a.m. and 2.05 p.m ?

(18) A cube has a volume of 64 cm³. What is its surface area ?

(19) Is the area of a stamp likely to be 4 cm², 40 cm² or 400 cm² ?

(20) Add the lowest even number below 200 to the highest odd number below 100.

Section B

(1) Ann spent one-third of her money. Later she spent another quarter of the original amount. This left her with £1.50. How much money did she start with ?

(2) When 15 is added to a number and the result is multiplied by 4 the answer is 96. What was the original number ?

(3) Study the following Venn diagram:

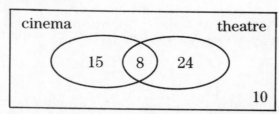

   (a) How many people were asked whether they enjoyed the cinema and theatre ?

   (b) How many of those questioned did not like the theatre ?

(4) A village increased its population between 1978 and 1988 by 20%. If its population in 1988 was 180, what was its population in 1978 ?

(5) Three bags of potatoes each weighed 8 kg. Two other bags of potatoes each weighed 13 kg. What was the average weight of a bag of potatoes ?

(6) A cuboid measures 3m × 6m × 9m.

   (a) Calculate its total surface area.

   (b) Calculate the total length of its edges.

Section C

(1) The following chart refers to the temperature in Marbella in the last week of July:

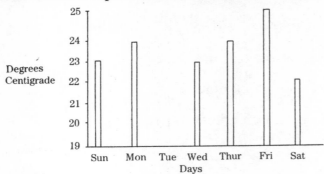

(a) The average daily temperature was 23 degrees. What was Tuesday's temperature ?

(b) If Tuesday's temperature had been 27 degrees, what would have been the weekly average temperature ?

(c) What day suffered the largest drop in temperature compared with the previous day ?

(d) Two days had cloudy afternoons. Which two days were these likely to have been ?

(2) What is a prime number ? Make six prime numbers using *all* the digits 1 - 9 inclusive, but use each digit only once.

(3) If you start with a number 2 and place an extra digit in front, you get 12 which is six times the number you started with.

(a) Which number, when an extra digit is placed in front of it, becomes three times greater than the original number ?

(b) Which number, when an extra digit is placed in front of it, becomes five times greater than the original number ?

(4) In a practical maths lesson a pupil is given a 7 litre jug, a 10 litre jug and a container which can hold 20 litres of water. There is access to a tap.

The task is to put *exactly* 9 litres of water into the container. Explain how this could be done.

(5) Two dice are thrown, one red and one blue. The "score" is obtained by doubling the number uppermost on the red and adding it to the number uppermost on the blue.

(a) What is the highest "score" that can be obtained ?
(b) How many "scores" are 12 or more ?
(c) How many "scores" are multiples of 3 ?
(d) How many "scores" are square numbers ?

MODULE THIRTY-ONE

Section A

(1) Add seventy nine to one hundred and sixty one thousand four hundred and ninety eight.

(2) Add the prime numbers between 20 and 40.

(3) Express 8.45 p.m. in 24 hour clock time.

(4) Find the area of a square whose perimeter is 20 cm.

(5) $37.409 + 61.73$

(6) $93.9 - 1.074$

(7) 93.74×5.4

(8) $93.002 \div 0.02$

(9) $3^4/_5 + 23^3/_4$

(10) $31^1/_5 - 2^3/_4$

(11) $2^1/_{10} \times 7^1/_7$

(12) $4^3/_8 \div 1^3/_4$

(13) $9 \div 10,000$

(14) How many fives in 25 ?

(15) Find the cost of 200 stamps priced 19 pence each.

(16) If today is Monday, 16th June, what will the day and date be in 80 days time ?

(17) 3.4 km + 5 m 5 cm

(18) 6 hours 17 mins − 3 hours 49 mins

(19) How many pieces of material 2 m 75 cm in length can be cut from a piece of material 275 m long ?

(20) Express 23,748 to the nearest thousand.

Section B

(1) The volume of a container is 300 m³. If its width is 8 m and its length is 15 m, what is its height ?

(2) Which is the larger amount and by how much: 27% of £600 or 0.2 of £1,000 ?

(3) In a group of girls, three-quarters played hockey and two-fifths played netball. If all the girls played at least one game and nine played both games, how many only played netball ?

(4) Jacqueline left home at 8.40 and arrived at school at 8.55. She walked an average speed of 6 km/h. The next day she ran to school, leaving home at 8.45 and arriving at school at the same time. What was the average speed of her run ?

(5) A child in an infant class was asked to write down all the numbers from 1 to 100. Instead of writing a 7 he wrote Γ. How many times did he write Γ ?

(6) Pat was asked to divide a number by 19 but instead she multiplied the number by 19. If her answer was 1,083, what was the correct answer to the question ?

Section C

(1) To find the sum of even numbers, it is possible to use the following pattern:

$$2= \quad 1 \times 2$$
$$2 + 4= \quad 2 \times 3$$
$$2 + 4 + 6= \quad 3 \times 4$$
$$2 + 4 + 6 + 8= \quad 4 \times 5$$

   (a) Write down the next line of the pattern.

   (b) Write down the right-hand side of the line when the left hand side of the pattern ends .... $+ 16 + 18$.

   (c) By using the pattern first find the total of the first 100 even numbers and the first 1,000 even numbers.

(2) To "kathryn" two numbers is represented by the letter "k". When two numbers are "kathryned" the first number is multiplied by itself, the number of times being the value of the second number. Thus $k63 = 6 \times 6 \times 6 = 126$.

   (a) What is the value of $k35$?

   (b) What is the value of x when $kx4 = 625$?

   (c) What is the value of x when $k4x = 256$?

   (d) What two digit number has the same k as k43 ?

(3) Stephen has a red disc with the number 5 printed on one side and 3 on the other. He also has a yellow disc with the number 4 printed on one side and 6 on the other side.

He throws the two discs in the air and they land on a table. He then totals the two numbers by adding them together.

   (a) How many different totals are possible ?

   (b) What is the difference between the highest and lowest totals ?

   (c) What is the probability (chance) that the total is a prime number ?

   (d) What is the probability (chance) that the total is an even number ?

(4) The following graph reflects Michael's cycle ride between his home and the coast:

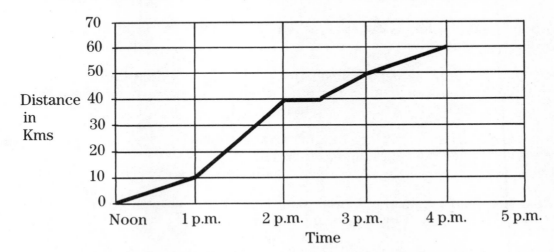

   (a) How far does Michael live from the coast ?

   (b) What was the average speed of the journey ?

   (c) For how long did Michael rest ?

   (d) During which hour did Michael cover the greatest distance ?

   (e) What was his average speed over the last 20 km to the nearest km.

MODULE THIRTY-TWO

Section A

(1) Reduce eleven thousand and nine by sixty seven.

(2) Add the square numbers between 100 and 200.

(3) How many minutes between 10.57 a.m. and 1.15 p.m ?

(4) Find the surface area of a cube of edge 3 cm.

(5) Reduce $3^3/_4$ to eighths.

(6) 17 hours 24 mins $\div$ 6

(7) Find the cost of 19 tickets if each ticket costs £9.50.

(8) $97.013 + 9.09$

(9) $36.47 - 2.009$

(10) 3.67×2.5

(11) $39.055 \div 0.5$

(12) $18^2/_3 + 3^3/_4$

(13) $31^1/_3 - 4^3/_4$

(14) $5^1/_{10} \div 1^2/_3$

(15) $5^1/_{10} \times 1^2/_3$

(16) On a map 1 cm represents 2 km. What area does 2 cm² represent ?

(17) How many cm in 0.03 km ?

(18) 3.4 litres + 96 ml.

(19) Add the lowest three digit odd number to the highest three digit even number.

(20) 9 hours 48 mins $\times$ 9

Section B

(1) The distance round a field is 240 m. If the length of the field is exactly double its width, what is the area of the field ?

(2) In a group of children at a party, one-quarter asked for Coca-Cola and one-third of the remainder asked for orange juice. The other children asked for milk-shakes. If 12 children asked for milk-shakes, how many were at the party ?

(3) Six of Ann's cakes had an average weight of 200 g. However, when she made six more, the average weight of all the cakes increased to 210 g.
What was the average weight of the second batch of six cakes ?

(4) In the summer maths exam, Peter and Emma scored 144 marks. If Peter scored 14 more marks than Emma, how many marks did Emma get ?

(5) Three pupils in one month received 38 merit marks. Emily obtained three times as many as Frederick, whilst John obtained five times as many as Emily. How many merit marks did they each receive ?

(6) By Christmas Eve, the price of turkeys had fallen by 20% compared with their price earlier in the week. If a turkey was priced £16.00 on Christmas Eve, what was its earlier value ?

Section C

(1) When you add or multiply two numbers together, it does not make any difference in which order the numbers are written. Thus $8 + 7$ and $7 + 8$ both equal 15, and 8×7 and 7×8 both equal 56. It is said that the operations of addition and multiplication are *associative*.

(a) Show whether the operations of division and subtraction are associative.

When the symbol † is placed between two numbers, it means both numbers are halved and then multiplied.

(b) Show whether $6 \dagger 5$ is an associative operation.

When the symbol § is placed between two numbers, it means double the first number and multiply the result by the second number.

(c) Show whether $8 \S 6$ is an associative operation.

(2) The "divo" of two numbers is how many times the first number can be divided by the second. So the "divo" (12,4) = 3, because 12 divided by 4 = 3. In each of the following, find the value of x:

(a) Divo $(25,x) = 10$
(b) Divo $(x,8) = 6$
(c) Divo (Divo $(36,x)$) (Divo $(18,x)$) = 2

(3) In reference to a cuboid, its length, width and height are said to be its dimensions.

When the dimensions of a cuboid are doubled its volume is increased eight times ($2 \times 2 \times 2$). When the dimensions of a cuboid are trebled, its volume is increased 27 times ($3 \times 3 \times 3$).

(a) If the dimensions of a cuboid are multiplied by 5, what is its increase in volume ?

(b) A container has a volume of 123 m³. When its dimensions are doubled, what is its volume ?

(c) A container's volume is 600 m³. The container is filled with packages 1 m by 2 m by 3 m. How many packages fit into the container ?

If the dimensions of the container are halved, how many packages would it then hold ?

(4) In this question a digit code has been used. Each digit has been replaced by another digit. Thus, 1 replaces 7 and 3 replaces 5.

Here are four sums in the digit code:

(a) $1 + 4 = 6$ (b) $9 - 8 = 8$
(c) $7 - 5 = 7$ (d) $2 - 3 = 0$

Use the above sums to work out what the other coded digits stand for and complete the table:

Code digit	0	1	2	3	4	5	6	7	8	9
Equivalent digit		7		5						

(5) In the Hale Open Tennis Competition, 128 players were invited to compete in the Singles Championship.

(a) How many matches would the winner play ?
(b) How many matches would be played in the entire Championship ?

67

MODULE THIRTY-THREE

Section A

(1) $3^3/_4 + 6^2/_7$

(2) $15^1/_3 - 2^4/_5$

(3) $1^2/_7 \times 9^1/_3$

(4) $3^1/_8 \div 3^3/_4$

(5) $9.7 + 15.36$

(6) $39.4 - 2.007$

(7) 39.89×2.5

(8) $15.003 \div 0.03$

(9) $9,876 \times 89$

(10) $951 \div 17$

(11) 9 hours 15 mins − 2 hours 39 mins

(12) 7 hours 49 mins × 9

(13) 27 hours 24 mins ÷ 6

(14) What is the value of 7 in 837.468 ?

(15) Express 101,003 in words.

(16) Find the value of 0.3 of £60.

(17) Add the prime numbers between 70 and 85.

(18) Find the cost of 36 articles if the price of 9 articles is £11.99.

(19) Find $2^1/_2$% of £60.

(20) What is the lowest three digit number 3, 5 and 18 will all divide into, giving a remainder of 1 ?

Section B

(1) Pat studied the 150 cars that passed by her house one morning. She discovered that 83 of the cars were British made and 103 of the cars were driven by women. What is the lowest number of British made cars that could have been driven by women ?

(2) A container 10 metres in length, $2^1/_2$ metres wide and 4 metres high was three quarters filled with boxes of bananas. If each box was a cube shape of edge $^1/_3$ m, how many more boxes could be put into the container ?

(3) David bought nine cans of paint at £14.00 each and 11 cans of paint at £18.00 each. What was the average price of each can of paint ?

(4) The price of a car was reduced by 10% to £8,100. At this reduced price it still did not sell so it was reduced by an additional 10% from the original price. What was the final sale price ?

(5) A cube's edges total 60 cm. What is the volume of the cube ?

(6) If Robert had an additional 11 Smarties, he would be able to give 37 children 17 Smarties each. How many Smarties did he actually have ?

Section C

(1) If two successive numbers are squared, the difference between the two numbers is always equal to twice the smallest, plus one. For example, 3 and 4:

$3^2 = 3 \times 3 = 9$

$4^2 = 4 \times 4 = 16$

$16 - 9 = 7$ which equals $(3 \times 2) + 1 = 7$

Complete the following pattern substituting the correct number for the missing letters.

$3^2 - 2^2 = 9 - 4 = 5: 2 \times 2 + 1 = 5$

$5^2 - 4^2 = 25 - 16 = 9: 4 \times 2 + 1 = 9$

$7^2 - 6^2 = a - b = c: d \times 2 + 1 = c$

$x^2 - y^2 = 121 - 100 = 21: y \times 2 + 1 = 21$

$R^2 - P^2 = Q - Z = 27: P \times 2 + 1 = 27$

(2) When a red coloured dice and a yellow coloured dice are thrown the "score" is the difference between the two numbers shown. How many different combinations will result in a "score" of 3 or more ?

(3) When two numbers are separated by the letter "S", the answer is the remainder when the sum of the two numbers is divided by 5.

For example, $8\,S\,9 = 2$ because $8 + 9 = 17$, and 17 divided by $5 = 3$ *remainder* 2.

(a) What is $17\,S\,19$?
(b) What is the smallest number that can replace x in $x\,S\,32 = 4$?
(c) What is the smallest number that can replace x in $x\,S\,x = 4$?
(d) What is the smallest two digit number than can replace x in $x\,S\,4 = 0$?

(4) In the following series, each number is eight more than the number before it.

(a) Give the next four numbers: $19 ; 27 ; 35$
(b) What is the first number in the series if the sixth and seventh numbers are 46 and 54 ?
(c) If the first number in the series is 5, what is the fiftieth number ?
(d) What is the difference between the hundredth and two hundredth number in any 8-series ?

(5) The number of Turkish stamps owned by Alan, Brian and Chris are in the ratio $8 : 7 : 5$. What fraction of the total number of stamps does Brian have ?

If Brian is given 10 stamps by Alan and 5 stamps by Chris, the ratio changes to $3 : 5 : 2$. What fraction of the total number of stamps does Brian now have ?

How many stamps were there altogether ?

MODULE THIRTY-FOUR

Section A

(1) Express six hundred and one thousand four hundred and nine in figures.

(2) Express $87\frac{1}{2}\%$ as a fraction in its lowest terms.

(3) $3\frac{4}{5} + 2\frac{6}{7}$

(4) $9\frac{1}{3} - 2\frac{4}{5}$

(5) $2\frac{1}{10} \times 5\frac{5}{7}$

(6) $8\frac{2}{5} \div 2\frac{1}{10}$

(7) $3.8 + 31.075$

(8) $9.7 - 3.095$

(9) 43.7×3.6

(10) $2.55 \div 1.7$

(11) Express the binary number 1010 in base ten (as a denary number).

(12) Express 23 in base two (as a binary number).

(13) Add the following binary numbers: $101 + 1111$.

(14) Carry out the following subtraction in base two: $1001 - 11$.

(15) Reduce $3\frac{3}{4}$ to eighths.

(16) 9 hours 39 mins $\times$ 7

(17) 9.7 km + 56 m

(18) Find the value of 0.19 of 400.

(19) Find the total cost of 9 tickets at £9.75 each.

(20) How many times can 17 be subtracted from 601 ?

Section B

(1) Vivienne bought nine ties at 3 for £2.99 and six pairs of socks at 3 pairs for £2.95. How much change would she receive from £20 ?

(2) Joe can swim 10 metres in $7\frac{1}{2}$ seconds.
(a) How long would it take him to swim 70 metres at the same speed ?
(b) How far would he swim in a minute at the same speed ?

(3) Pat sprinted one-quarter of the distance, jogged one-third of the remainder and then walked the final 4 km.
What was the total distance covered ?

(4) A plastic container of volume 1 cubic metre holds 1,000 litres. How many containers of water are needed to fill a rectangular bath measuring 6 metres long and 2 metres wide, to a depth of $1\frac{1}{2}$ metres ? How many litres of water would be in the bath when it was completely filled ?

(5) In a group of 60 men, 37 watched Grandstand and 43 watched Saturday Night Theatre. What fraction of the group watched both Grandstand and Saturday Night Theatre ?

(6) A house priced £100,000 in 1988 increased its value by 20% in 1989 and again in 1990. What was the value of the house at the end of 1990 ?

Section C

(1) Three numbers are called a "Derby trio" when the second number is $1\frac{1}{4}$ times the first number, while the third number is $1\frac{1}{2}$ times the first.
For example: 40 50 60 form a "Derby trio".

Three numbers are called a "Liverpool trio" when the second number is $1\frac{1}{5}$ times the first number and the third number is $1\frac{1}{2}$ times the first.
For example, 50 60 75 form a "Liverpool trio".

(a) Find a "Derby trio" when the first number is 80.
(b) Find a "Liverpool trio" when the second number is 96.
(c) Find a "Derby trio" whose first number is the second number of a "Liverpool trio" which starts with 120.

(2) One way of sorting out a list of names into alphabetical order is to interchange neighbouring pairs which are in the wrong order.

From the above, it can be seen that the largest number of interchanges that might be needed to put three names into alphabetical order is three.
Using the same method, what is the *largest* number of interchanges that might be necessary to put five names into alphabetical order ?

(3) If you have a square shape, by putting a pin in its centre, it is possible to turn the square four times, each time changing the position of the corners, but not seeming to change the appearance of the square.
This can be shown in the following four diagrams:

How many times can you rotate the following two shapes without changing their original appearance ?

(a)
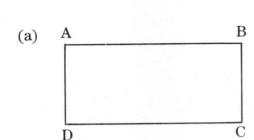

(b)
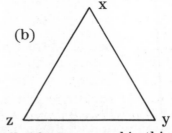
(Nb. All sides are equal in this triangle)

(4) Billy always kept his 1 pence and 2 pence coins. One day he counted his money and found he had a total of 14 pence.

Write out the various combinations of 1 and 2 pence coins he could have which would give him a total of 14 pence.

71

MODULE THIRTY-FIVE

Section A

(1) Express six hundred and five thousand four hundred and ten in figures.

(2) What number multiplied by 19 results in 988 ?

(3) 3 hours 53 mins + 4 hours 39 mins

(4) 6 hours 39 mins − 2 hours 48 mins

(5) 9 hours 49 mins × 7

(6) 15 hours 24 mins ÷ 6

(7) £37.9 × 17

(8) $9^3/_4 + 2^2/_5$

(9) $9^1/_3 - 3^4/_7$

(10) $2^5/_8 \times 4^4/_7$

(11) $12^1/_4 \div 2^5/_8$

(12) 19.3 + 0.376

(13) 9.7 − 2.001

(14) 3.17 × 2.5

(15) 6.46 ÷ 1.9

(16) Reduce $3^1/_2$ to quarters.

(17) Add the prime numbers between 1 and 19.

(18) Express 8.30 p.m. in 24 hour clock time.

(19) How many minutes between 11.40 a.m. and 2.15 p.m ?

(20) How many cm^2 in $^3/_4$ m^2 ?

Section B

(1) A container measuring 6 m by 4 m by $2^1/_2$ m is half filled with water. How many litres of water are in the container ? (1 m^3 = 1,000 litres)

(2) Add the following binary numbers, leaving your answer in base two:
101 + 1101 + 11.

(3) The average temperature on the first two days of a test match was 24 degrees Centigrade. If the first day was 4 degrees hotter than the second day, what was the temperature on the second day ?

(4) It took 12 men 180 days to paint a bridge across the River Seventeen. How long would it take ten men assuming that all the men work at the same rate ?

(5) On a map the scale is 1 : 100,000. The distance between two towns is $5^1/_2$ km. How many cm would this be represented by on the same map ?

(6) Find the total cost of 9 apples at 3 for 41 pence and 15 oranges at 5 for £0.93.

Section C

(1) When Gillian was appointed as an assistant in a record shop, she was given a choice as to how she wanted to be paid. She could either receive a weekly wage of £145 or a basic pay of £100 per week plus 75 pence bonus for every compact disc she sold.

    (a) In one week she decided to receive the weekly wage of £145. During that week she sold 45 compact discs. How much did she gain or lose by her decision ?

    (b) The following week she changed her method of payment and earned a total of £161.50. How many compact discs did she sell during the week ?

    (c) During one year when she was paid for 52 weeks at a salary of £145 per week, she sold 2,500 compact discs. How much better or worse off would she have been if she had decided to be paid on the bonus system ?

(2) How many different rectangles can be made by joining the dots in the diagram below ?

          .   .   .   .

          .   .   .   .

          .   .   .   .

          .   .   .   .

(3) A van carrying 120 packing cases, all of equal weight, has a total weight of 1,920 kgs. When half the cases were delivered, the total weight was reduced to 1,560 kgs. The maximum total legal weight of the van and cases is 2,200 kgs. What is the largest number of cases that can be carried ?

(4) In the following "arthog" dart board, there are three separate areas: inner, middle and outer. Any dart in the outer area scores double, any dart in the inner area scores treble.

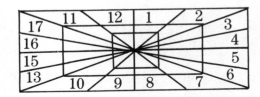

    (a) What is the highest possible score with three darts hitting the board ?

    (b) What is the lowest possible score with all three darts scoring, but all in different numbers *and* different areas.

    (c) Alan scored one with his first throw. After three more throws his score had increased to 15. Write out six ways in which this score could have been achieved.

(5) A penny is tossed four times. How many different combinations of heads/tails are possible ?

MODULE THIRTY-SIX

Section A

(1) 978×38

(2) How many sixths in 36 ?

(3) How many times can 17 be subtracted from 697 ?

(4) Add the even numbers between 80 and 90.

(5) Find the value of 0.9 of 880.

(6) $9\frac{7}{8} + 2\frac{3}{4}$

(7) $9\frac{1}{3} - 4\frac{3}{4}$

(8) $2\frac{7}{10} \times 1\frac{2}{3}$

(9) $4\frac{3}{8} \div 7\frac{1}{2}$

(10) $3.4 + 9.007$

(11) $13.1 - 2.096$

(12) 15.3×2.4

(13) $8.8 \div 0.002$

(14) Find 15% of 40.

(15) If today is Tuesday 15th July, what will the day and date be in 113 days time ?

(16) Find the perimeter of a square given that its area is 36 cm².

(17) Find the cost of 36 articles if 9 cost £15.07.

(18) 3.4 km + 59 m

(19) 5.3 kg − 98 g

(20) How many millilitres in 3.4 litres ?

Section B

(1) It takes a mechanical digger 45 seconds to remove 1 m³ of earth. How long would it take to dig a trench 50 m long, 1 m wide and $2\frac{1}{2}$ m deep ?

(2) From 1101 subtract 11 when both numbers are in base 2. Leave your answer in base 2.

(3) John, Peter and Paul had £66.00 between them. John had half as much as Peter, whilst Paul had eight times more than John.
How much did they each have ?

(4) If 60 bottles of milk can provide drinks for 150 people, how many people would 144 bottles of milk provide drinks for ?

(5) In a group $\frac{3}{4}$ said they enjoyed trifle and $\frac{3}{5}$ said they enjoyed gâteau. If 14 of the group enjoyed both trifle and gâteau, how many only enjoyed trifle ?

(6) In a race a sprinter completed the last ten metres in one second. What was his speed over the last 10 metres, expressed in km. per hour ?

Section C

(1) The following rectangle has its measurements in Base Three.

```
┌──────────────────────┐
│      120 cm          │
│112 cm                │
│                      │
└──────────────────────┘
```

Calculate (a) its perimeter (b) its area.
Give both answers (i) in base 3, and (ii) in base 10.

(2) In the following question, when * is placed between two numbers, it means write out the remainder when the sum of the two numbers is divided by 5. For example, 7*6 = 3 because 7 + 6 = 13 and 13 divided by 5 = 2 remainder 3.

   (a) What is 11*47 ?
   (b) What is the lowest possible missing number when 17*x = 4
   (c) When x is greater than 10, what is the lowest value of x when x*8 = 4?
   (d) When x is a number between 10 and 20, what is the value of x when (7*x)*1 = 0 ?

(3) Set A is a series of two digit numbers formed by using no other digits but 1, 2, 3, 4 and 5.

   (a) How many numbers are in Set A ?
   (b) How many numbers in Set A are prime numbers ?
   (c) How many numbers in Set A are multiples of 5 ?

Set B is a set of multiples of 5 between 1 and 1,000.
   (d) How many elements are there in A´B ?

(4) Six counters, three white and three black, are placed in a straight line in the following order:

It is required to move all the black counters to the right, thus obtaining the following order:

By only interchanging neighbouring counters, show the lowest possible number of moves required to do this.

(5) One coach left London at 12 noon travelling north to Manchester. At 12.30 p.m. a coach left Manchester, travelling to London. Both coaches were travelling exactly the same route. The distance between London and Manchester is 214 km. The coach leaving London averaged 80 km/h and the coach leaving Manchester averaged 65 km/h.

(a) At 1.18 p.m. how far apart were the two coaches ?
(b) At what time did the two coaches meet ?
(c) How far from London were the coaches when they crossed ?

MODULE THIRTY-SEVEN

Section A

(1) Express six hundred and one thousand two hundred and nine in figures.

(2) What is the value of the 8 digit in: 38,493 ?

(3) What must be added to 901 to make it exactly divisible by 19 ?

(4) Reduce $3\frac{1}{2}$ to eighths.   (5) How many fifths in 25 ?

(6) $3\frac{4}{5} + 2\frac{5}{7}$ (7) $8\frac{1}{3} - 2\frac{3}{5}$

(8) $3\frac{2}{11} \times 2\frac{1}{5}$ (9) $6\frac{1}{9} \div 8\frac{1}{3}$

(10) $3.7 + 9.009$ (11) $3.4 - 1.097$

(12) 9.7×4.05 (13) 7 hours 36 mins + 5 hours 49 mins

(14) 3 hrs 17 mins − 1 hr 39 mins   (15) 9 hours 24 minutes × 9

(16) 33 hours 24 minutes ÷ 6   (17) Express 3.4 km in metres.

(18) Find the volume of a cube of edge $\frac{1}{3}$ m. Express your answer as a fraction of a cubic metre.

(19) How many minutes are there between 11.05 am and 2.35 pm ?

(20) £39.75 × 15

Section B

(1) What is the lowest number into which 24, 66 and 165 will all divide without there being any remainder ?

(2) A boy is half the age of his father, and a quarter the age of his grandfather. If their total ages amount to 154 years, how old is the grandfather ?

(3) A pool measuring 8 m by 12 m is surrounded by a path 1 m wide.
What is the area of the path ?

(4) A pupil studying for an exam read an average of 37 pages of notes for five nights, and then 56 and 49 pages over the weekend. If his notes consisted of 400 pages exactly, how many pages did he still have to read ?

(5) In still water, John can row at an average speed of 16 k/h.
If he rowed against a current running at 4 k/h for 2 hours 15 minutes, what distance would he have covered ?

(6) Pat achieved a score of 38 marks out of 40 in a maths test.
Express her result as a percentage.

Section C

(1) Steven had two dice, one yellow and one red. He threw both dice at the same time, his score being the sum of the two uppermost faces.

    (a) How many different throws could produce a score of 10 or more ?

    (b) How many different throws could produce a score of 5 or less ?

    (c) How many of all the separate possible scores are prime numbers ?

    (d) How many of the possible scores are multiples of three ?

(2) Study the following diagram of a cuboid:

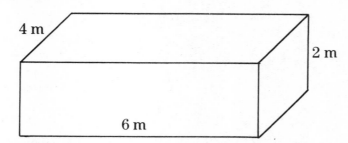

4 m   2 m   6 m

    (a) Calculate the volume of the cuboid.

Each of the measurements is now doubled.
(b) Calculate the volume of the enlarged cuboid.

Each of the measurements is now doubled again.
(c) Calculate the volume of the further enlarged cuboid.

    (d) From the three results you have obtained, work out what effect it has on the volume of a cuboid, when each of its measurements is doubled.

(3) When a number is "foxed", it is multiplied by the next number after it, and then divided by two.
So, when 9 is "foxed", the answer is 45, because $9 \times 10 = 90$, and $90 \div 2 = 45$.

    (a) "Fox" 11.
    (b) When a number is "foxed" the result is 120. What is the number ?

(4) To find the "DAS" of a binary number, the number is first converted into base ten. The converted number is then added to the original *digits* of the binary number, *as if* it were a denary number.
For example: "DAS" 1011 = 11 (the denary equivalent) + 1011 = 1022.

    (a) Find "DAS" 11011

    (b) Find "DAS" 111100

    (c) The "DAS" of a number is 10018; what is the number ?

MODULE THIRTY-EIGHT

Section A

(1) 976×345

(2) £$39.05 \div 5$

(3) Add together all the multiples of three between 10 and 20.

(4) If $x^2 = 400$, what is the value of x ?

(5) If $\dfrac{x}{4} = 20$, what is the value of x ?

(6) $7^1/_3 + 21^3/_4$

(7) $10^1/_3 \div 2$

(8) $4^3/_8 - 1^3/_4$

(9) $2 \times 1^2/_3$

(10) $3.086 - 2.1$

(11) $8.37 + 91.36$

(12) 3.76×2.6

(13) $15.072 \div 0.03$

(14) 3.4 km. + 54 m.

(15) 3.7 km. ÷ 5

(16) How many litres of petrol can be piped into a storage tank measuring 4 m by 3 m by $1^1/_2$ m ?

(17) How many times can 17 be subtracted from 619 ?

(18) Find the value of 0.7 of £630.

(19) $3.7 \div 1000$

(20) 9.4 kg. − 59 g.

Section B

(1) A piece of paper measuring 20 cm by 15 cm has a three cm square cut out of the middle. What fraction of the original paper remains ?

(2) One 12 litre container is half filled with water, and half filled with oil.
Another 12 litre container is $^1/_3$ filled with water, and $^2/_3$ filled with oil.
Both these containers are then emptied into a 24 litre container.
In the larger container, what fraction is filled with water, and what fraction is filled with oil ?

(3) A man 1.6 m tall finds that his shadow is 1.2 m long. He is standing next to a tree the shadow of which is 18 m long.
What is the height of the tree?

(4) A metal girder 39 m in length was cut into two sections, so that one piece was 7 m longer than the other. How long was the shorter piece ?

(5) The area of a rectangle is 108 cm. If its length is three times its width, find its perimeter.

(6) After relegation, a football team's average attendance fell by 20% to 24,000.

What was the average attendance before relegation ?

Section C

(1) In the following **figures** calculate the value of x. You are given the information that the angles of a triangle add up to 180°, and the angles of any four-sided figure add up to 360°.

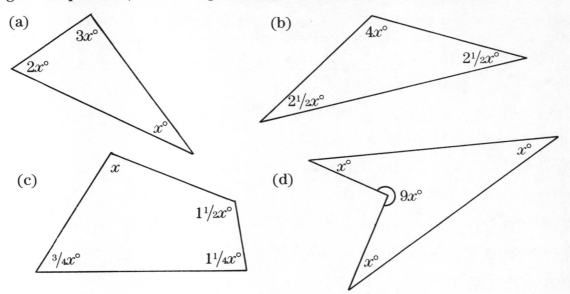

(a) $3x°$ $2x°$ $x°$

(b) $4x°$ $2\frac{1}{2}x°$ $2\frac{1}{2}x°$

(c) x $1\frac{1}{2}x°$ $\frac{3}{4}x°$ $1\frac{1}{4}x°$

(d) $x°$ $x°$ $9x°$ $x°$

(2) The following is a diagram of a MODDAY CLOCK.

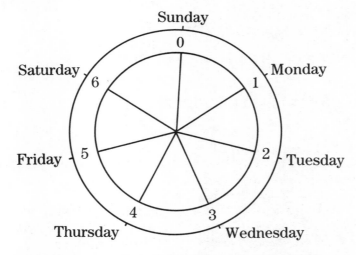

Sunday
0
Saturday 6 · 1 Monday
Friday 5 · 2 Tuesday
4 3
Thursday Wednesday

If you start on Sunday, and want to know the day in four days' time, you simply read the day beside number 4 – which is Thursday.
If you start on Wednesday, and want to know the day in 30 days' time, you add the 30 to Wednesday's number (3), making 33. Then divide by 7, and read off the remainder, which gives you the answer.
$33 \div 7 = 4$ remainder 5 – and Day 5 is <u>Friday</u>.

(a) If today is Monday, what day will it be in eight days' time ?
(b) If today is Thursday, what day will it be in 80 days' time ?
(c) If today is Friday, what day will it be in 98 days' time ?
(d) Explain why 7 is the number you divide by in your calculations.

(3) Draw up a diagram of your own to represent a MODMONTH CLOCK, showing months instead of days.
Briefly explain how you would calculate the month in 40 months' time.

INDEX

Problems on the topics set out below will generally be found in the Section B parts of the Modules referred to. There may also be simpler questions in Section A.

The investigative questions in Section C cannot readily be classified. Accordingly references to Section C (prefixed with C) are only included in a few specific instances.